MW00387442

THE LODGE OF THE BODHISATTVAS

AND THE QUESTION OF THE 20TH CENTURY BODHISATTVA

A CONTEMPORARY READING AND PRESENTATION OF NEW IDEAS

Filip Filipov

Preslav Pavlov

Translation edited by Edward Schuldt

© First edition: Filip Filipov, Preslav Pavlov, *authors 2007*

© Second English edition: Preslav Pavlov, *author and publisher 2018*

E-book mobi ISBN 978-619-228-038-3

   PDF   ISBN 978-619-228-037-6

All rights reserved. No part of this book may be reproduced in any form without the written permission of the authors, except for brief quotations included in critical reviews and articles.

i

Introduction

The book now lying in your hands holds a challenge to the Anthroposophical Movement to take up once again the Bodhisattva Question. That question is: In what human being did the Maitreya Bodhisattva appear in the twentieth century?

This became a consuming topic of discussion among pupils of Rudolf Steiner during parts of the first half of the twentieth century, both before and after the founding of the Anthroposophical Society. Its significance can be judged by two statements Rudolf Steiner made in 1911: that "humanity must gain the capacity... to see the supersensible Christ, and for that the spiritual scientific movement is there. That is its mission: to create the conditions that bring about an understanding for the Christ, in order then to make it possible to see the Christ;"[1] and that the Maitreya Bodhisattva "will be the real herald of the Christ in etheric raiment."[2]

---

[1] Rudolf Steiner, *Esoteric Christianity and the Spiritual Guidance of Humanity* (GA 130), Mailand,
21 September 1911. As Sergei Prokofieff comments in The East in the Light of the West, Part Three,
p. 415, the instances of Rudolf Steiner's remarks making this point "could be multiplied without any difficulty," for example: "Without books and documents, this great event, the reappearance of the Christ, stands there for those who worthily prepare themselves for it. And it is the duty of Anthroposophy to proclaim this" (Hannover, 10 May 1910, in The Event of the Christ Appearance in the Etheric World (GA 118).
[2] Rudolf Steiner, *Esoteric Christianity and the Spiritual Guidance of*

Yet today this question of the identity of the Maitreya and the teachings he gave the world has all but disappeared from the minds of the members of the Anthroposophical Movement, even to the extent that the concept of a bodhisattva is unfamiliar to many.

Bodhisattvas, Rudolf Steiner explained, are human beings who follow a path of development different from the rest of humanity. They are at home in the World of Providence, a plane of existence lying between Devachan and Nirvana. Twelve of them gather around the Christ and receive from Him the impulses that they bring in turn as teachings to humanity.[3] Bodhisattvas are not born into bodies as are the rest of humanity, but incorporate into a human bearer, as the Christ incorporated into Jesus of Nazareth at the Jordan. The Bodhisattva Question is therefore one of finding which historical personality became the bearer of the Bodhisattva in the twentieth century.

At the end of his path of teaching humanity over many incorporations, a bodhisattva becomes enlightened and is elevated to buddhahood; so it was that, in the sixth century B.C., the Gautama Bodhisattva became the Gautama Buddha. Since that time, the bodhisattva who has been most active within humanity, incorporating once every hundred years, is the Maitreya Bodhisattva.

Humanity (GA 130), Leipzig, 5 November 1911.
[3] Rudolf Steiner, *The Christ Impulse and the Development of Ego-Consciousness* (GA 116), Berlin, 25 October 1909.

His particular task, as Rudolf Steiner indicated, is leading humanity towards an experience of the Etheric Christ.

Already in 1909, Rudolf Steiner underscored the importance of knowing and understanding what the bodhisattvas have to say who follow the Christ, the first of them being the Maitreya.

> *The last of these messengers [sent by the Christ to prepare his physical appearance on the earth] was the Buddha, who brought the teaching of compassion and love. Yet there were previously other bodhisattvas, and after Christ there will be other bodhisattvas who will have to develop that which has come to the earth through the Christ Jesus. It will be good if human beings listen to the bodhisattvas who come after, for they are His servants.... Therefore we say that the Christ sent the bodhisattvas in advance to prepare humanity for Him; and He sends them afterwards so that the greatest deed of the evolution of the earth can be better and better understood.*[4]

Rudolf Steiner spoke of the Maitreya Bodhisattva often between 1909 and 1912, the period during which he was also speaking about the return of the Christ in the etheric. Among much else about the Maitreya, Rudolf Steiner said, "[H]e is also incorporated now."[5] From

---

[4] Rudolf Steiner, *The Deeper Secrets of Human Evolution in the Light of the Gospels* (GA 117), Zurich, 19 November 1909. This lecture is not yet translated into English.

misinterpretations of that statement have issued some of the many misconceptions and false claims regarding the personality in whom the Maitreya appeared in the twentieth century.

In the first part of the this study, Preslav Pavlov and Filip Filipov present a comprehensive overview of what Rudolf Steiner has had to say about the Maitreya Bodhisattva, particularly the characteristics by which we can distinguish him from false Maitreyas. The exactitude of this overview makes it possible, in the second part, to discredit as false every possible Maitreya that has been put forward to date. The false Maitreyas that will be most familiar to the reader include Krishnamurti, brought forward within the Theosophical Society in the first decade of the last century; Rudolf Steiner, whom Adolf Arenson claimed in 1930, five years after Steiner's death, was the Bodhisattva;[6] and Valentin Tomberg. In each of these cases, and in many others, Pavlov and Filipov show, at the hand of Rudolf Steiner's statements, how none of them can reasonably be taken as the bearer of the Maitreya Bodhisattva in the twentieth century.

There have been two notable occasions in the last thirty years in which anthroposophical authors writing in

---

[5] Rudolf Steiner, *Esoteric Christianity and the Spiritual Guidance of Humanity* (GA 130), Leipzig, 5 November 1911.

[6] Published online in German at https://www.anthroweb.info/geschichte/geschichte-ag/sukzession-und-falsche-bodhisattvas/arenson.html; retrieved August 2017.

English have turned to the Bodhisattva Question. The first of these is a short passage in volume three of Sergei Prokofieff's *East in the Light of the West*, in which he concludes that the Maitreya Bodhisattva inspired Rudolf Steiner in the period 1909-1912 but was unable, because of the difficult conditions created by the claim of the Theosophical Society regarding Krishnamurti, to incorporate into a human bearer.[7] The second is *The Bodhisattva Question*, in which Thomas Meyer addresses the entire matter thoroughly. Meyer's primary concern is to show as false the claim first put forward publicly in 1930 (though it had by then already had currency within the anthroposophical circles for twenty years) that Rudolf Steiner himself was the bearer of the Maitreya Bodhisattva. This claim was disputed immediately by Elizabeth Vreede, who delivered two lectures opposing Aronson's reasoning and conclusions. It was Aronson's lectures, however, that were printed many times over and circulated widely within the Anthroposophical Movement, while Vreede's were ignored and forgotten. It is one of the great services of Meyer's book to make Vreede's lectures[8] available to a wide audience for the first time.

---

[7] See Prokofieff, *The East in the Light of the West*, Part Three, pp. 447-453.

[8] Also published online in German at https://www.anthroweb.info/geschichte/geschichte-ag/ sukzession-und-falsche-bodhisattvas/vreede.html; retrieved August 2017.

Meyer draws no conclusion regarding the historical personality who bore the Maitreya, as he is unable to provide an answer to the central question that he poses in his introduction: "Who," he writes, "apart from Rudolf Steiner, has attempted... to proclaim the 'reappearance of the Christ in the etheric spiritual realm'?"[9] In the third part of this book, Pavlov and Filipov give the answer: Peter Deunov, the Bulgarian spiritual teacher who lived from 1864 to 1944 and was also known as the Master Beinsa Douno.

It is characteristic of Pavlov and Filipov's very methodical approach that they open the third part of the book by narrowing the time and place in which the Maitreya could have appeared. Regarding the time, they rely, among other indications, on Rudolf Steiner's comment that the Maitreya was already incorporated when Rudolf Steiner was speaking about him. Considerations of place, however, must rest on reasonable surmise: it is reasonable to surmise, they write, that the Maitreya would appear in a place where Christianity had already been established for a very long time in order to provide fertile ground for the reception of the Maitreya's teaching; and it is reasonable to surmise, from Rudolf Steiner's lack of direct comment on the place in which the Bodhisattva was incorporated, that

[9] Meyer, T.H. *The Bodhisattva Question*, p. 3. Forest Row, 2010: Temple Lodge Press.

the Maitreya was active in an area that did not overlap with the geography of Rudolf Steiner's own activity.

This argument, while being a logical step in Pavlov and Filipov's method, is perhaps the least forceful part of their work, as it is grounded neither in cold historical fact nor in pure clairvoyant insight. Yet the path of reasoning to arrive at the idea that it is in Eastern Europe, and specifically Bulgaria, in which the Maitreya should be sought has great merit as an exercise in itself and as a model for similar research.

The strongest support of the thesis that Peter Deunov was the bearer of the Maitreya Bodhisattva in the twentieth century comes, however, in response to Thomas Meyer's question: Who besides Rudolf Steiner proclaimed the reappearance of the Christ in the etheric? Once Peter Deunov began his spiritual teaching, he spoke often about the Etheric Christ, and Pavlov and Filipov provide compelling examples of this teaching, among which are these:

There is no epoch in human history when Christ worked like this. Today, Christ works most of all. Several centuries ago, Christ was above, in the highest worlds, but now He has descended lower, into the astral and etheric worlds, closer to the material world. Two great events will take place: first, the Spirit of Christ will begin revealing itself in human beings; certainly, this will start with advanced souls. When you experience a fine, unselfish feeling, you experience compassion, love, mercy, and this indicates that the Spirit of Christ has dawned in you and starts working within. The Apostle Paul says too, 'It is no longer I who live, but Christ lives in me.' [10]

People who expect Christ to be born again as a young child are people with a wrong outlook. Christ was born and keeps being born in the hearts and souls of people. Nowadays, Christ cannot be borne by a woman. If you expect the coming of the Redeemer, open your souls, He will be born there. Moreover, Christ is being born simultaneously in many people. When Christ is born in your soul, you will be useful both to yourself and to the people around you. This is Resurrection. This is the awakening of the human soul. When Christ lives in people's souls, everyone will become alive, will rise and join hands like brothers. [11]

[The] Christ is coming now to visit human minds and hearts.... When we say that Christ is coming now, some think that He will come from the outside. Christ will not come from the outside. He will not appear either in human or in any other form whatsoever. When the

___

[10] From conversations with the Master Peter Deunov published by Boyan Boev in *The Good Predisposition,* chapter entitled The Master about Christ, ISBN 954-744-026-8. Available in Bulgarian only.

[11] Peter Deunov, *The Awakening of the Human Soul,* a talk from the volume *He was Examining Them,* The Sunday talks series 1923.

rays of the sun enter your home, does this mean that the sun has visited you? Remember that Christ is a manifestation of the love of God. And He will come as an internal light in the minds and hearts of people. This light will draw everyone around Christ as a great center. The opening of human minds and hearts and the reception of Christ within—this will be the Second Appearance of Christ on the earth.[12]

The reader acquainted with the work of Rudolf Steiner can experience, at the hand of these short excerpts, the difference in the approaches of Peter Deunov and Rudolf Steiner in speaking about spiritual matters. That difference is significant and can pose challenges for pupils of Rudolf Steiner who have cultivated in themselves a feeling for spiritual-scientific exactitude. Rudolf Steiner spoke out of forces of enlightened thinking warmed by the heart; Peter Deunov speaks directly from the heart. His words are not scientifically exact and spare as are Rudolf Steiner's, and we might experience this with some distaste upon an initial reading. Looking beyond that difference and setting aside our inclination towards the scientific, however, and entering into Peter Deunov's words as they are in themselves will be well rewarded: we will find in

---

[12] From *The Master Speaks*, compiled by Georgi Radev (following texts of Master Beinsa Douno), in the chapter entitled Christ. ISBN 954-8785-17-X. Available in Bulgarian only.

them the message of a herald of the Etheric Christ who lived and worked at the same time as Rudolf Steiner.

Pavlov and Filipov outline the possibility of a synthesis of the thinking-centered approach of Rudolf Steiner and the heart-centered approach of Peter Deunov. They are themselves examples of this synthesis, having immersed themselves for decades in both streams. This immersion is a path to realizing Rudolf Steiner's aim of bringing warmth to thinking and light to moral feeling and thereby coming closer to perceiving the Christ in the etheric.

This book opens for the first time a particular gateway to accomplishing that goal. As spiritually striving human beings in our time, we are concerned not only with the facts of spiritual science as Rudolf Steiner laid them out a hundred years ago, but with the unfolding of spiritual life as it is occurring today and the way in which spiritual life works into earthly life. We are concerned not only with the impact of evil, focused as we may be on the incarnation of Ahriman and the appearance of the Anti-Christ, but also with the ongoing life and work of those human beings who are leading the development of human spirituality towards beholding the Etheric Christ, among them Rudolf Steiner, Christian Rosenkreutz, and Parzival, as well the individuality whom Rudolf Steiner described as "the true herald of the Christ in etheric raiment," the Maitreya Bodhisattva.

Whether Peter Deunov was the bearer of the Maitreya Bodhisattva in the twentieth century is a question that each reader must consider for him- or herself. *The Lodge of the Bodhisattvas and the Question of the 20th Century Bodhisattva* presents a cogent, detailed argument that he is; but we owe it to the authors of this work as well as to ourselves to examine the case they make as thoroughly and as critically as we can.

Behind the question of the possible appearance of the Bodhisattva in Peter Deunov stands a larger one: How do we find the Maitreya Bodhisattva? Rudolf Steiner's statements that "the task of the spiritual scientific movement is to cultivate the conditions in which human beings can behold the Etheric Christ" and that the Maitreya Bodhisattva is "the true herald of the Christ in etheric raiment" may awaken us to the inner task of finding the Bodhisattva. This is not a matter of satisfying mere curiosity: it is a matter of establishing a living inner connection with the Bodhisattva that can help lead us through our heart's power of seeing into the immediate presence of the Etheric Christ.

Edward Schuldt
Durham, North Carolina, USA
Easter 2018

Foreword

This book is a new attempt to address a question that has, since 1911, interested every anthroposophist seeking the truth, namely: As which personality did the Maitreya Bodhisattva appear in the 20th century? For the last one hundred years, this question has been examined many times from various points of view; throughout that time, it has remained relevant as well as controversial. On the one hand, this book provides a survey of the most prominent research done to date; on the other, it offers a completely new thesis on this question.

The Maitreya Bodhisattva, according to Rudolf Steiner, is that great spiritual Master* who comes to teach humanity to recognize the Christ in His etheric reappearance in the astral world; this is the Master bringing Christ's power and life to awareness in humanity. Therefore, this question can be well taken to heart by every anthroposophist seeking and following the Michael impulse.

In dealing with a task so central to the life of Anthroposophy and anthroposophists, one that demands such responsibility, bearing as it does so strongly on the future of humanity, questions inevitably arise regarding a method of research that

---

*In this book, we use the term "Master" to refer to members of the Lodge of the Bodhisattvas as well as the Lodge of the Masters/Mahatmas.

will ensure that one maintain one's common sense and does not deviate from the path of truth. How can each person, using his or her clear and rational consciousness, together with the rudiments of his or her imaginative perception, recognize the hidden but active Bodhisattva among us? The research approach set out in this book is based on several distinct methods arising from Anthroposophical spiritual science and inspired by the Michael impulse of our time. All of them are intended to provide a methodology for recognizing the appearance of the Maitreya Bodhisattva in the 20th century, a methodology which should be clear and concrete, with no trace of any atavistic clairvoyance. This approach, described in detail in the following "Note Concerning Research Methodology", can be generally summarized in the following way: voluminous research in spiritual-scientific esoteric texts, accompanied by spiritual-scientific analysis and comparison of information; developing a working hypothesis and thesis by applying the principles of correspondence and analogy in an environment of free imaginative meditation and imaginative-inspirative revelations; comparative analysis of the newly formulated ideas on the basis of the Christ-Lucifer-Ahriman model; critical analysis and verification of each hypothesis and thesis in a working group; and cause-and-effect observations of the life realized through the spiritual environment constructed by each new idea.

The first impulses of the new thesis stated in this book date back to the spring and summer of 1994. Later, during the following seven years, the idea was slowly and systematically investigated, and in 2001 was publicized for the first time among wider anthroposophical circles. During this seven-year period of ripening, sources of both a material and a spiritual nature were investigated. Only then did the authors of this book find themselves sufficiently ready to share this idea with the wider public. Thus, in December 2002, they delivered the first public lecture when they announced and explained their new ideas. Certainly the difficulties and contradictions accompanying every innovative impulse were not long in appearing. Due to the spiritual and public scope of the idea, people in Bulgarian circles connected strongly to this question, considered the impulse a personal possession, and embarked on an aggressive campaign to impose it upon their audience. Rushing to achieve a sensational effect quickly, they relied on atavistic mediumistic sources and tried to compromise the essence of the thesis. On the other hand, fierce and non-scientific comments of a fundamentalist character generated from other circles did not take long to surface.

This book represents an attempt to challenge these negative tendencies by a clear methodology, firmly rooted in Michaelic spiritual-scientific impulses that can help clear away delusions thriving on rumors and fantasies. Led by their striving for immediate inspiration from the Maitreya Bodhisattva, the authors have endeavored to put forward a new idea in a pure and spiritual-scientific style, where the freedom of individual perspective and will are sacred, so that all anthroposophists seeking a Michaelic, free spiritual-scientific impulse can gain knowledge regarding this question and make additional and deeper research on their own.

The historical personality investigated in this book is well known in Bulgarian spiritual circles. Due to the language barrier and the Cold War of the past several decades, however, this personality has remained little known in the wider anthroposophical world. Thanks to the spreading of the Michael impulse through the process of the attempted European integration, we find ourselves in a new era confronting the spiritual world and us with new responsibilities. With this book, the authors are attempting to bridge the European East and West spiritually and culturally, thereby taking a further Michaelic step in spreading esoteric Christianity throughout the world and within humanity.

Regardless of the personal conclusions at which every reader will arrive, the authors of the book are grateful for the time their readers take in their search for the truth.

Preslav Pavlov
Varna, September 2006

P.S. This book is a result of the joint effort of the two authors: Filip Filipov and Preslav Pavlov. Filip Filipov mainly documented and collected the spiritual-scientific research of Preslav Pavlov. The edition of the original, Bulgarian, version was made jointly by both of them.

A Note Concerning Research Methodology

We believe it necessary to explain at the outset the spiritual-scientific methods applied to the ideas presented here as they have been received and developed further by us. These steps are followed in sequence, with the last leading back to the first:

(i)   the investigation and research of esoteric texts on a large scale;

(ii)   spiritual-scientific analysis and the comparison of the information collected;

(iii) formulating summarized theses and theorems;

(iv)   applying the principle of correspondence and analogy under the conditions of free imaginative reflections. The culmination of this process is the reception of inspirational thoughts and ideas of a new nature in terms of quality (not imaginative and inspirative consciousness of the purest kind but rather first steps taken in this direction);

(v)   reflection, discussion and verification of the newly gathered information in a group as well as delivering of lectures and preparation of seminars and discussions in a wider circle on the themes and ideas that have been developed;

(vi)   observation of the causes and consequences in the life arising out of the newly established spiritual-scientific environment;

(vii)   targeted monitoring to ascertain whether the newly developed ideas serve the centralizing Christ principle or the polarizing Luciferic and Ahrimanic influences and whether the newly developed ideas serve the cosmopolitan aims of Michael of achieving a unified and global common human spirituality centered in Esoteric Christianity.

With regard to references: for the sake of maximum precision and accuracy, when giving information found in Rudolf Steiner's anthroposophical work, the location is referenced by the GA (Gesamtausgabe, collected works) number and the date of the lecture. When a new thesis is stated, one that has been received after intensive work through the method described above, it is marked by an asterisk [*]. This is done solely in the name of Michaelic freedom and the scientific approach to spirituality under the contemporary circumstances in this epoch of the Consciousness Soul. The team developing the ideas presented here does not aim to impose them in any way upon readers with anthroposophical interests; on the contrary, the team has a humble hope these ideas will be considered as an attempt for individuals to enter freely into the widths of the spiritual-scientific ocean of contemporary esoteric Christianity.

For a more thorough understanding of our work, we recommend that our readers follow up each footnoted reference by reading the original content in the respective GA volumes. This will also help avoid misleading conclusions and forestall doubt when following the logical path of our research.

Preslav Pavlov

The Lodge of the Bodhisattvas and the Question of the 20th Century Bodhisattva
A contemporary reading and presentation of new ideas

The impulse to become aware of our own essence is that recursive vortex which transforms us into beings endowed with an 'I'.[1] As the Ancient Greeks bequeathed to us the familiar saying *Know Thyself,* so has Parsifal woven into our souls the question: *What is the secret of the Grail?* Two thousand years after the Turning Point of Time and a century after Anthroposophy entered European culture, the striving towards self-knowledge has not faded but rather transformed into a spiritual science. In this work we shall, inspired by the legend of the questing Parsifal, take the liberty of putting forward questions out of our inquiring souls and to chisel out of our 'I' the anticipated form of the Holy Chalice.[2]

These two questions form the objectives of this article:

What is the organization of the White Lodge of the Masters of humanity[3] and what is its activity in the present?

What is the structure of the human 'I'?

This is in fact once more the question of 'I'-hood, but now in its macrocosmic and microcosmic aspects. The Christ Jesus and His sacrificial deeds are the deepest essence of the Macrocosmic 'I'-hood,[4] which gradually becomes an ever-growing 'I'-hood of humanity as a whole. Just as a human being has an individual 'I', similarly the whole of humanity forms a complete organism* which finds its organizing center in the 'I' of the Cosmos.[5] As we become acquainted with the structure of the human 'I', we shall come to know the essence and the activity of the White Lodge as well. Conversely, by examining the activity of the Christ Being and His heralds, the Masters of humanity, we shall also gain a deep knowledge of our own essence.

If we contemplate the structure of the human 'I' by applying the methods of Spiritual Science, we can discover a double twelvefoldness*. The twelve senses

---

* As described in the foregoing Note Concerning Research Methodology, for the sake of maximum precision and accuracy, when delivering information sourced from an anthroposophical work, it is referenced by the collected works (GA) number and the date of the lecture. When a new thesis is stated, received after intensive work under the above-mentioned methods, it is marked by [*]. This is done solely in the name of the Michael freedom and the scientific approach to spirituality under the contemporary circumstances in the epoch of the Consciousness Soul. The team developing the present ideas does not aim to impose them in any way upon the readers with anthroposophical interests; on the contrary, the authors hope that they will be considered as an attempt for a free and individual entering into the wide space of the spiritual-scientific ocean of the contemporary Esoteric Christianity.

described in detail by Rudolf Steiner[6] link the human 'I' with the objective, outer world, the macrocosmos.[7] At the same time, the very intimate, internal structure of the microcosmic 'I' itself is also divided into twelve. The human being can thus be understood as a center with a double periphery. The center of the human 'I' is the spark of God, imparted by the macrocosmic 'I'– the Christ,[8] so that the human 'I' is a result and a projection of the Macrocosmic 'I' of Humanity. The human 'I' is surrounded by an inner periphery structured similarly to the twelve-sign Zodiac: three basic members (consciousness soul, intellectual soul, and sentient soul), each having four internal functions.[9] To summarize: The human being has twelve senses represented in the outer periphery, and inside that an internal microcosm of the 'I' containing the twelve internal functions. In the center of whole is the projection of the macrocosmic 'I' – Christ. This is the very essence of the human 'I'.

We are led then to the questions:

Does the Cosmic 'I' of Humanity have a similar organization? If so, what view does Spiritual Science have of this matter?

It is clear from indications given by Rudolf Steiner[10] that there is a Lodge of Twelve Masters[11] who long ago traveled the path before which humanity now stands. We know, concerning these Masters of humanity, that there are, at any given time, seven actively incarnated on the physical plane, while five remain in the spiritual world. The incarnated Masters often appear in the world as ordinary people, but they bear sublime virtues and work toward one sacred purpose: that humankind should be able to apply in everyday life the Wisdom streaming from the Holy Spirit in the name of Christ. In these written answers Rudolf Steiner mentioned the following names: the Master Jesus; Kuthumi; Moriah: Illarion: and Saint-Germaine (Christian Rosenkreutz).

On the other hand, Rudolf Steiner talks also about a still more lofty Lodge consisting of twelve human beings at the Bodhisattva level of development.[12] These exceptionally advanced human beings inhabit the World of Providence, the Buddhi-plane lying above the Higher Devachan, and contemplate the Christ Being directly.[13] They are intensely connected with the spiritual world and only partly with the physical one.[14] They have a specific mission to humankind related to an ever more profound knowledge of the Christ Being.[15] Currently one of these Bodhisattvas, the Maitreya Bodhisattva, has a special mission on Earth and is to become the first Enlightened One, the first Buddha after Christ. Five thousand years after receiving the tiara of Wisdom from the Buddha, the tiara of the Holy Spirit, the Maitreya will make the final step from the Bodhisattva to Buddha, through permeating human life and culture with a mighty moral force arising from Christ's *power and life*.[16] Rudolf Steiner talks specifically about several Bodhisattvas. Scythianos, Zarathustra, and Gautama[17] worked upon humanity in their successive missions and have passed from the Bodhisattva level to that of Buddha. It was already mentioned that the current Bodhisattva works upon humanity and assumed the mission of being a herald of the Holy Spirit on Earth after Guatama. His mission started approximately 600 years before the Turning Point of Time. In a series of lectures, Rudolf Steiner also speaks about the Bodhisattva Apollo, manifested through Orpheus, who had a special mission for the development of the human soul through music.[18] According to Elizabeth Vreede,[19] and according to the architectural imagination imparted by Rudolf Steiner in the interior of the small dome of the First Goetheanum, it can be stated that six of the Bodhisattvas appeared prior to the Mystery of Golgotha and six will appear after.[20]

So, we can outline the following idea*: The White Lodge of the Masters of humanity is one unified whole. This unified spiritual organism is structurally similar to the human 'I' because this Lodge is in itself the very principle of 'I'-hood of humanity.[21] Thus the whole, in its totality, projects its fractal model onto its parts, by forming the so-called *golden* (solar) *mean.* In other words, the principle of macrocosmic 'I'-hood, the very 'I' of humankind as a whole, has a structure similar to the 'I' of the human being. If the human 'I' has a double twelvefoldness expressed in the twelve senses and the twelve internal spiritual functions, then the 'I' of humankind has a double twelvefoldness expressed, correspondingly, in the Lodge of the twelve Masters-Mahatmas and the Lodge of the twelve Great Masters-Bodhisattvas.

This leads to a further question:

The human 'I' has its own intimate center, which has a direct link with the Christ Being. What is the analogous center of the macrocosmic 'I' of humankind?

The intimate center of the 'I' of humankind is the Nathan Soul[22] which was separated and saved from the Luciferic temptation during Lemuria. It is the soul-mate of all humanity, the soul-mate of the first Adam. Penetrating it, Christ performed his sacrifices for the sake of the salvation and advancement of the human race. When considering the Lodge of the Bodhisattvas, we can contemplate it as an intimate part of the 'I' of humanity, one more internal organism of the White Lodge. The Lodge of the Bodhisattvas is the very soul of humankind*, the living zodiac surrounding and elevating the hierarchy of humanity, a zodiac permeated by the Holy Spirit[23] and organized around the sacrificial activity of Christ through the soul-mate of the first Adam. The soul of the Nathan Jesus and the twelve Bodhisattvas are one whole, just as the center and periphery of the circle form a whole that cannot be separated.[24]

It should be noted that it would be a great mistake to identify the Lodge of the twelve Masters-Mahatmas (The Master Jesus, Kuthumi, Moriah, Illarion, Christian Rosenkreutz, etc.)[25] with the Lodge of the twelve Bodhisattvas (Scythianos, Zarathustra, Gautama, Apollo, Maitreya, etc.).[26] If such a mistake is allowed, it would amount to arguing that the twelve senses and the twelve internal functions of the human 'I' are the same thing, which is utterly incorrect. It can be said that the primary source of a similarly wrong conception will be found in the interpretation given by Hella Wiesberger (in her addendum "The Masters of Wisdom" included in GA 264), who assumes that Master Jesus (Master Zarathustra) is the Bodhisattva who has completed his mission and risen to Buddha before the beginning of the mission of the Bodhisattva who became the Gautama Buddha. In this way, she makes the ranks of masters (Master-Mahatma and Bodhisattva-Buddha) equivalent in the sense that they are all Masters of humanity. However, by doing so, she overlooks the fact that these Masters come from different levels of development and their ranks are, indeed, not equal.[27]

Examining the question concerning the essence of a Bodhisattva being, one may fall under another specific delusion, deriving from the Oriental point of view, which does not emphasize the development of the human 'I'. Based on various understandings of *GA 110* (17.04.1909), the concepts of the *Bodhisattva* being and

7

of the *Archangel* being are taken as exactly identical or virtually equivalent. To avoid any misunderstanding in this direction, we quote once more Rudolf Steiner's words: *...a Bodhisattva is a human being who is continually connected with the spiritual world and not living completely in the physical.*[28] Moreover, *[When] one...is called a Bodhisattva, that means a human being who has sufficiently taken into himself...the Buddhi [the Life-Spirit, the Buddha principle]*[29] *of the Earth.*[30] Therefore the concept of *Bodhisattva* designates a certain stage in human development. Rudolf Steiner states, *When such a being becomes a Bodhisattva, Buddha, or Master, this signifies an inner development, just a higher one, that every human being can go through. An esoteric schooling of the human being is just a beginning of that which leads to becoming a Buddha*[31] [as a stage of development].

The correct understanding of a Bodhisattva's mission requires a clarification of the major characteristics in their manifestations during the Fifth post-Atlantean Epoch. According to Spiritual Science, the twelve Great Masters send one representative who manifests the impulses of the Holy Spirit. It can be said that he guides human development for a period of approximately 5000 years.[32] During this period, he reincarnates in a very particular way approximately every 100 years.[33] The process of the Bodhisattva's reincarnation can be explained in the following way:

these human beings, because of their supreme and special evolution, experience the need to be continually in touch with the supreme spiritual worlds; because of this they cannot penetrate deeply into the physical world and be born as ordinary humans. For this reason they use other human beings and incorporate into their spiritual essence. The people who are thus bearers of Bodhisattvas are themselves highly initiated human individuals. A peculiar feature in the lives of the Bodhisattvas is that they remain unknown to the world until they reach the age of thirty.[34] Part of the Bodhisattva's 'I' incorporates into the bodily structures, prepared in advance, of the human bearer at approximately thirty-three years of age. A radical change of personality can be witnessed.

Rudolf Steiner gives a number of significant characteristics by which it is possible to recognize the Bodhisattva being, which we will now describe.

The first particular characteristic of a Bodhisattva, manifested through the human bearer, is that he stands seemingly alone in the world, not related to any Master-Disciple chain. His word is of extraordinary moral power, because the Bodhisattva, due to the particular incorporation into the human bearer, succeeds in sustaining constant contact both with the spiritual field of the Higher Devachan and with the even loftier World of Providence, from where the great principles and virtues of the Christ Being spring. This process of exchange with human beings on the physical level occurs periodically until the Bodhisattva develops the ability to build a human body on his own and thus to be born as a human being in his own body. This incarnation is also the last time the Bodhisattva appears in a physical body.[35] The need to incarnate physically is completed simultaneously with the end of the specific mission of the Bodhisattva to humanity. It is then said that the individual Bodhisattva has reached the Buddha level of development.

Generally speaking, the mission of a Bodhisattva is intended to foster the development of particular characteristics, virtues and strengths in humanity, which correspond to the innermost essence of the individual Great Master-Bodhisattva. Only some of the incarnations of the Master-Bodhisattvas have become known historically. When a Bodhisattva completes his mission in his last incarnation, he rises from the Bodhisattva level to that of Buddha and passes on the leadership to a new herald of the Lodge of the Holy Spirit, the Lodge of the twelve Bodhisattvas.[36] In this last incarnation, the teaching of the Bodhisattva, having reached the level of Buddha, envelopes humanity as a whole. This is further enabled by the fact that he has prepared a sufficient number of disciples who perceive the eternal Wisdom of Christ streaming from Him.

It is worth remembering that the twelve Great Masters contemplate the image of Christ directly and are bearers and heralds of the Word of Christ.[37] They are the closest Disciples of Christ, the souls who were the first to make the deepest and most complete relation with the Spirit of Christ as early as ancient times. The question of the contact process between the Christ Being and the twelve Bodhisattvas, of the formation of this loftiest lodge in the spiritual history of the Solar system and, more precisely, in the esoteric history of the Earth, is the topic of another work.

As already mentioned, the Bodhisattvas could be called Masters of the Divine Wisdom — bearers of the Daylight streaming from the Christ Being. Their mission is to bring the Divine Wisdom of Christ to our world. They do this through their teaching, through which people are able to understand the Christ Being at a higher level. What can be said about the Buddhas is that they are no longer bearers of a given teaching but become, so to say, wellsprings of the Christ Life[38] and thereby extend their mission throughout the entire Solar System.

The second singular characteristic of the Bodhisattvas is that, while each has a main human bearer, they do not always act only through that one. In this same way, other great beings can also be called to a certain extent Bodhisattvas, but, in such cases, the complete manifestation of the Bodhisattva does not occur as it does with the main human-bearer. Rudolf Steiner explains, for instance, that Hermes can in a certain way be called a Bodhisattva, even though the Bodhisattva was incorporated only to an extent in Hermes.[39] Moreover, during the time of a particular physical manifestation, when the Bodhisattva has already incorporated into a certain human individual, he can also inspire and guide other people sufficiently advanced in their initiation.[40] This is a manifestation of the spiritual power of the Great Masters of Wisdom.

Another characteristic particular to the Maitreya Bodhisattva is his relationship to the world-creative word. If we focus on the current stage of the activity of the Lodge of the Bodhisattvas, we should say that, following the advancement of the Gautama Bodhisattva to Buddha, the time had come for another Bodhisattva to assume the mission to humanity. This is the Maitreya Bodhisattva, who after another 3,000 years will become, so to say, the first Christian Buddha. Then, according to Rudolf Steiner, he will be manifested among human beings as the greatest Master of the Christ Impulse, who will work through the moral power of the Word.[41] Rudolf Steiner emphasizes that the name *Maitreya* means *the one who brings the Good through the Word.*[42] This Word will have a magical effect upon the will of people and will help them attain Christian virtues. *In the Maitreya Buddha, we are given the greatest teacher who has come to make clear to humanity the Christ-Event is its full scope. What is particular to him is that he, as the greatest teacher, will bring the most exalted word, the highest word.*[43] Rudolf Steiner spoke the remarkable words: *And if there would be for him [the Maitreya] a John the Evangelist, he would have to speak differently than John the Evangelist spoke of the Christ. Then it was said: "And the Word became Flesh"; the Evangelist John of the Maitreya Buddha would have to say: "And the Flesh became Word."*[44] Also that *the peculiarity about this Maitreya Buddha is that he should have to imitate, in specific way, what happened at Golgotha.*[45] This will be a specific characteristic feature during the preparation and manifestation of Maitreya-Buddha's mission.

Gautama Buddha completed his mission about 600 BC and gave humanity *the Wisdom stemming from Compassion and Love.* He entered a world called Nirvana but at the same time took from himself the tiara of the Holy Spirit and gave it to the Bodhisattva who succeeded him. And about a hundred years before the incarnation of the Solar Logos on the Earth, the Maitreya Bodhisattva is already known historically in his manifestation through the leader of the Essenes, Jeshu ben Pandira. Rudolf Steiner makes it clear in his book Esoteric Christianity (GA 130) and more precisely in his lecture from 5 November, 1911, that the Bodhisattva Maitreya was *that individuality who was then, a hundred years before Christ, incarnated as Jeshu ben Pandira as the herald of the Christ in the physical body. He is now that Bodhisattva of humanity until, in another three thousands years, he will advance from Bodhisattva to Buddha. Since then, he has incorporated nearly once every hundred years, he is also incorporated now and will be*

13

the actual herald of the Christ in etheric raiment, just as he then prophesied the Christ as the physical [the physical manifestation of] *Christ.*

It can be said that, in articulating these words, Rudolf Steiner implicitly assigns a personal task to each true disciple starting along the path of the spiritual science of Anthroposophy. Achieving this primary task will directly impact the correct understanding and realization of the appearance of Etheric Christ in the soul of those seeking the truth. This is because the Maitreya Bodhisattva, revealing himself during the first half of the 20th century, had, at the same time, a specific relationship to manifesting Christ's mission in the astral world. Rudolf Steiner gives a hint about this relationship in the words: *he is also incorporated now and will be the actual preacher of the Christ in etheric raiment.* Any awakened researcher of Esoteric Christianity will benefit from paying special attention to these prophetic words of Rudolf Steiner, if one seeks earnestly from the bottom of one's soul a cognitive path to the reappearance of Christ in the Etheric. Since the Maitreya Bodhisattva, preparing his mission, is *the greatest teacher that has come to make clear to humanity the Christ-Event is its full scope* and since he *is also incorporated now*, the anthroposophist seeking the radiance of the reappearance of the Christ in the Etheric will naturally ask the question: **How can I find the Maitreya Bodhisattva as he manifested physically in the 20th century and thereby also his**

contemporary teaching? Finding that teaching will provide a critically needed perspective on the contemporary manifestation of the Christ and is, in its essence, the third objective of this study. We shall try to deliver a very clear answer to that question in this work.

Due to a number of esoteric, ethical, and social considerations, Rudolf Steiner could not directly point to the name of the individual in which the Maitreya Bodhisattva appeared. On the other hand, through numerous clairvoyant revelations, signs, and instructions from the esoteric history of humanity and certain spiritual and scientific theorems, Rudolf Steiner seems to have sketched the image of Christ's herald, leaving it to us to complete this spiritual-historical picture, and thus to take essential steps into Esoteric Christianity. It is our view that we are, in this way, assigned a new task similar to the Quest for the Grail, a task that consists of seeking and finding the Word of the Maitreya Bodhisattva, the Herald of the Holy Spirit in 20th century. In order for us to reach the full depth of this esoteric research, we have to examine the spiritual path traveled so far towards this sublime aim. For this reason, we offer a survey of the attempts that have been made to answer the new Grail Question of our time.

A survey of hypotheses published to date regarding personalities known to history

***through which the Maitreya Bodhisattva may have
manifested in 20th century.***[46]

(1) The passage quoted above from the volume
Esoteric Christianity makes it clear that Maitreya
Bodhisattva was incarnated, or, more precisely,
incorporated, in 20th century and specifically at the time
of Rudolf Steiner. He says unambiguously, *The
Bodhisattva is also incorporated now and will be the
actual herald of Christ in etheric raiment.* When
someone is a herald in the name of the Christ, and
particularly when that herald is announcing the
Reappearance of the Christ Being in the Etheric, it is
essential that history not fail to rake notice of him. Apart
from this, there have long been certain prophesies about
the new appearance to humanity of the Great Master who
succeeded the Buddha. Perhaps this brought about the
first clearly unsuccessful attempt to discover the physical
manifestation of the Bodhisattva today: Annie Besant and
Charles Leadbeater believed that the Divine Being of
Christ and the human being of Maitreya were one and the
same thing. Furthermore, they announced that the new
World Master, who according to them is Christ and
Maitreya simultaneously, appeared in the young Indian
man named Krishnamurti. The power of intelligence and
light in the personality of Rudolf Steiner and the Spiritual
Master appearing in Bulgaria through Peter Deunov
(Beinsa Douno) worked against this reckless irrationality.
In a number of his lectures and at Theosophical

conferences, Rudolf Steiner spoke out against the temptation of the opposing spiritual powers to believe such an error; the Master Beinsa Douno (Peter Deunov) sent a letter to the same effect to Krishnamurti by a personal courier (Magdalena Popova).[47] Soon after this, Krishnamurti publicly denounced the allegations made about him, namely that he was to become the *New World Master*. The willingness of Annie Besant and Charles Leadbeater to *select a human being* as the coming World Master was in and of itself an act against the spiritual world driven by pride and ignorance. The Maitreya Bodhisattva, guided by Christ, chooses himself where and in whom he will appear.

It takes Humility to find the Grail!

(2) In the contemporary cultural epoch, humanity is making substantial steps towards the maturity of its 'I'-hood. After the mysteries of Golgotha, Christ changed the paths of initiation forever. He transformed the hierarchical relation of *Master* and *Disciple* into one of brotherly friendship. Even more, Christ, as the center of the human 'I', brought and radiated the *Consoling Rays* of *the Spirit of Truth* into our microcosm – *the Master* promised to us by the Lord; this is no longer only something external but something internal. However, spiritual maturity is needed to understand this new aspect of the mystery of Esoteric Christianity. Without that maturity, human thought will be liable to falling prey to temptation.

As an example of this temptation, we may look at a purely psychological aspect of this fundamental problem in the deeds of the Theosophical leaders, namely their inability to discern the internal structure of the White Lodge. They do not have an understanding for the Lodge of the Twelve Bodhisattvas living in direct contemplation of the Divine nature of Christ, who is the center of this Lodge. In their imagination, the Theosophists confuse and confound the *center* and the *periphery* of the White Lodge. This is most likely due purely to methodological reasons: in the present Michael epoch, where the spiritual freedom of the human 'I' is of critical significance, mediumism is a completely inadequate and even utterly dangerous approach to the spiritual world. This method of research clashes with the occult hygiene of the 'I'-hood and transforms human beings into easy prey for dark occult powers.

Falling into the trap of mediumism and the occult dictation of pseudo-mahatmas, the Roerich family made the following unsuccessful attempt to know the World Master Maitreya. Helena Roerich articulated the idea that there are three Bishops of the World – Buddha, Christ, and Maitreya, where Maitreya is the *Senior* one, the *First* and the *Last* among them, and apart from this he is the *King of Kings* and the *Master of Masters*.[48] As Helena Roerich explained it, the Maitreya Bodhisattva had long ago accomplished Enlightenment, had become Buddha and needs no physical incarnation, and naturally he is manifested as a Bishop of the Himalayan Shambhala.[49] Here we are evidently dealing once more with another aspect of the problem mentioned above. The error committed by Helena Roerich is analogous to a scientist researching the physical properties of light who looks through a prism for the first time, sees the prism dividing the light into rays of color, and thinks that the prism is prior to and more significant and substantial than the light itself. Helena and Nicholai Roerich, the founders of Agni Yoga, were in a similar situation: they exaggerated the image of the Master Maitreya, not being able to discern that he is a pure and sacred bearer of Christ's power and life. Because of this, and due to the fact that they were under the influence of Oriental occultists who clearly did not understand the depth of the Christ Being, they reached such a level of delusion that they found themselves in total conflict with the classic Buddhist predictions about the deeds of the Maitreya Bodhisattva and also with the revelations of anthroposophical spiritual science on the same question.

It takes Discernment to find the Grail!

(3) Towards the end of Rudolf Steiner's earthly path and immediately afterwards, research was begun within anthroposophical circles to investigate the enigma of Steiner's prophecies concerning the Maitreya Bodhisattva. On the one hand, it is clear that not knowing the identity and the teachings of the herald of the Christ in the 20th century implies a real and serious danger of

not attaining a complete understanding of the Etheric Reappearance of the Christ.[50] On the other hand, significant information is being accumulated about the Maitreya Bodhisattva's mission as a result of the examination and analysis of Rudolf Steiner's works. Through these efforts, it becomes clear that for a certain period Rudolf Steiner was under the direct inspiration of the Maitreya Bodhisattva.[51] Moreover, it becomes evident that Rudolf Steiner, in his conversation with Friedrich Rittelmeyer (August 1921), hinted that the one who appeared in Jeshu ben Pandira had, at the beginning of the century, already been born. A new hypothesis came about, according to which Rudolf Steiner himself is the successor and manifestation of the Bodhisattva in 20th century.

This thesis holds no promise because many Anthroposophists find sufficient evidence to the contrary. For instance, Sergei Prokofieff, in his work *The Birth of Christian Esotericism in the Twentieth Century and the Occult Powers that Oppose It* (vol. III of *The East in the Light of the West*), p. 95, emphasized that *any identification of Rudolf Steiner's individuality with the individuality of Bodhisattva Maitreya would be a gross mistake. Rudolf Steiner himself made twice very definite statements regarding this matter in response to questions put to him during [his lecture cycle on the Gospel of Matthew in Bern, September 1910] and shortly afterwards in Berlin.*

Any Anthroposophist who is familiar with spiritual-scientific terminology and aware of its distinctions and is involved in systematic and consequent research of anthroposophical sources knows that the terms *incorporation* and *inspiration* stand for two completely different concepts. Rudolf Steiner explicitly stated: *The Bodhisattva is also incorporated at the present and will be the actual herald of Christ in etheric raiment* which makes clear that he was referring to the incorporation at that time of the Maitreya Bodhisattva in another human individual. It would be vain and unhygienic in an occult sense for Rudolf Steiner to speak about the Great Master of our contemporary epoch if he had actually had himself in mind as well as entirely out of character for a man whom we know as a paragon of humility and morality. A thesis of this sort is founded on an obvious conceptual misunderstanding, but this does not make it less dangerous. Its danger lies in the fact that a misconception substantially similar to the truth undermines morality, in this case the moral basis of the Anthroposophy founded by Rudolf Steiner.

Elizabeth Vreede provides another substantial argument against the hypothesis that identifies Rudolf Steiner as the personality bearing of the Maitreya Bodhisattva. She pointed strongly in two of her lectures, published in *The Bodhisattva Question*,[52] to the idea that if one assumes that Rudolf Steiner is, in fact, the Bodhisattva, then an important phenomenon should have been witnessed, stated by himself during his lifetime as a major point, namely that a radical transformation of his consciousness should have taken place between his 30th and 33rd year. Since no such profound change was witnessed, one can draw the firm conclusion that it would be a mistake to adopt such a hypothesis. Another argument following this line of reasoning is that Rudolf Steiner wrote his own biography, and this shows the fluid and uninterrupted processes of his life and unambiguously points out that there has been no radical change around his 30th year – and therefore there are no grounds to argue that he, proclaiming the mission of the Bodhisattva in 20th century, actually meant himself. Although these comprehensive and significant arguments absolutely rule out such an idea, there remain people today who continue to support this dangerous idea.[53]

The Grail seeker needs pure thought!

(4) The statement of Rudolf Steiner in August 1921 concerning the birth of the Bodhisattva around the turn of the century confronts the seeking members of the Anthroposophical Society with another serious trial. That has to do with the personality of Valentine Tomberg (1900-1973). During his youth, he was an Anthroposophist, applying a spiritual-scientific research approach, but at about 40 years of age he left the Anthroposophical Society and adopted a serious Catholic-Jesuit orientation. The trial consists in the fact that at the first cursory glance it seems that one observes

the phenomenon mentioned by Rudolf Steiner characteristic of the Bodhisattva of 20th century: a person, born exactly at the beginning of the century, involved in esoteric-mystical deeds, and changing his convictions radically. For quite some time, wide esoteric circles have supported the view that it is precisely Tomberg who is the expected Bodhisattva.

This idea exhibits a peculiar materialism concerning spiritual and esoteric issues in that the so-called birth of the Bodhisattva is sought from a conventional-human point of view. Rudolf Steiner stated very explicitly the esoteric characteristic that the 20th century Bodhisattva will not be born the way human souls are born in the ordinary course of development, but that he will be incorporated in an elevated personality at about its 30th to 35th years of age, whereas this personality will undergo a radical change in the texture of its consciousness. This statement makes it immediately clear that if one looks for the so-called *birth of the Bodhisattva* at the beginning of 20th century, one should under no circumstances expect a baby to be born at about 1900. On the contrary, one should be looking for a person who is supposed to have reached the age of 33 at about 1900, i.e. a person born approximately during the period 1864-70; moreover, this should be precisely a person with a radical change both in the spiritual basis of consciousness and lifestyle at about the beginning of 20th century.[54] Obviously the rough and inadequate identification of the personalities of the incorporating Spiritual Master at the *Bodhisattva* level with a human individuality, who is his bearer, leads to the materialistic hypothesis that the 20th century Bodhisattva will be 33 years of age in 1933.

If we accept that the being manifested through Jeshu ben Pandira was born again at the beginning of the century, and if we follow Rudolf Steiner's theses logically, it will be understood that it is the incorporation of the Bodhisattva into his human bearer that must have taken place at about the beginning of the century. Valentine Tomberg did indeed have a peculiarly split life, but the change in his spiritual concepts and orientation took place when he reached the age of 40, when the two parts of his life virtually exclude each other. It is beyond doubt that Anthroposophy and its ideas have nothing to do with the esoteric activity of the Catholic Church and even less with Ignatius Loyola, the founder of the Jesuit order and of one of the inspirers of Valentine Tomberg. There are even suggestions that Tomberg was in fact under the occult influence of secret Catholic circles.[55]

We can also address this thesis indirectly with the following question: since Rudolf Steiner's legacy is several hundred volumes of written and spoken work providing both a highly articulated conceptual framework and a path of inner schooling for understanding humanity's relationship to the spiritual worlds and the true Christianizing of human culture, what could we expect would be the legacy of the 20th century Bodhisattva, who works in an even more direct relationship with the Christ? And do we find any similarity between what we would expect to find as the Bodhisattva's legacy and the work of Valentin Tomberg? We definitely cannot do so because his works are within much narrower limits than one would expect from a Bodhisattva, while methodologically his work was focused upon the Catholic-Jesuit teaching and meditations in relation with the Tarot cards. And in the end, according to the material presented in the epilogue of Prokofieff's *The Case of Valentine Tomberg*, it is evident that he specifically and clearly distances himself from any identification whatsoever of himself with the personality bearing the Maitreya Bodhisattva.

Even in the worst of internal battles against split-mindedness and doubts, the seeker of the Holy Grail remains devoted to one's goal, and the Grail protects the seeker from the darkest beasts!

(5) Another hypothesis concerning the appearance of the Bodhisattva in 20th century is also analyzed rather superficially in *The Case of Valentine Tomberg*.* Christian Lazaridès, one of the authors, asserts that there are circles that see the 20th century Bodhisattva in the

---

* The authors are referring to the 1995 German first edition of *Der Fall Tomberg*. This includes an essay by Christian Lazaridès that was omitted from the second German edition and therefore does not appear in the English translation published in 1997 by Temple Lodge Press as *The Case of Valentine Tomberg.* — Ed.

person of Mihail Ivanov, known as Omraam Mikhaël Aïvanhov. This is founded in the personal speculations of certain individuals belonging to the French organization called *The Universal White Brotherhood*, speculations lacking any consistent spiritual-scientific thinking. Without substantial argument or serious grounds, Lazaridès mentions that *occult brotherhoods, having the task to substitute the impulse of the Bodhisattva, try to implement this task by presenting various persons, provided there are some coincidences with the well-known biographical information of the current bearer of the impulse.*[56] The author links this accusation to the White Brotherhood and overtly indicts a spiritual society, different in essence but close in terms of ideas, to the spiritual Anthroposophical Society.

To take up this issue, we must first provide an answer to the question: *Who is Omraam Mikhaël Aïvanhov?* Mihail Ivanov was a progressive Bulgarian born in 1900 in the present-day Macedonia, who at an early age had serious spiritual interests including Anthroposophy. He met the Master Peter Deunov, known by his spiritual name as the Master Beinsa Douno, in Varna in 1917, and became one of his followers. He took part in the spiritual life of the Esoteric Christian School founded by the Master Peter Deunov in 1922, who led two twenty-three-year long esoteric classes within the School. In 1937, under the direct guidance of the Master Peter Deunov, he immigrated to France. In 1953, in

Bonfin, he founded *'Fraternité Blanche Universelle'*, which by its ideal and universal structure is similar to the spiritual society called *Brotherly Chain* founded in Bulgaria by the Master Peter Deunov; this society had as its ideal the ten Hierarchies of Christ (from the intelligent human souls to the Brothers of Love, the Seraphim), which Master Peter Deunov called the *Universal White Brotherhood*. The Head of this live organism of Hierarchies of Light is Christ.[57] In 1959, Mihail Ivanov visited India, met Babaji and, although he assumed the Sanskrit sounding spiritual name of Omraam Mikhaël Aïvanhov, he remained devoted to the impulse received from the Master Peter Deunov. Until the end of his earthly path in 1986, he worked intensively as lecturer; he has thousands of followers, while the esoteric Christian form of Paneurhythmy given by his Master, Beinsa Douno, is practiced in dozens of countries.[58]

Going into these specific details, it can be seen immediately that people who see the 20th century Bodhisattva in the person of Mihail Ivanov, as well as people commenting on this matter who accept the proposition that the Bodhisattva must be born in the ordinary human way at the beginning of the century, make a gross mistake due to a simple lack of knowledge about the descriptive spiritual characteristics presented by Rudolf Steiner. As do other commentators, they confuse and identify the personality of the human bearer with the personality of the Bodhisattva (who is also human, but very far advanced). Both Valentin Tomberg and Mihail Ivanov were born in 1900, and this has misled quite a few people who do not know the results of anthroposophical spiritual scientific research regarding the Bodhisattva. Nevertheless, in the case of Mihail Ivanov another fact is of a much greater significance: throughout his work and in his speeches, he continually emphasized that he had had a spiritual Master and that this was the Master Peter Deunov. Moreover, a deeper reading of his lectures makes it immediately clear that the essence of the lectures represent a personal interpretative and creative point of view in comparison with the word of the Master Peter Deunov (Beinsa Douno). Many elements and ideas are borrowed by Mihail Ivanov from the word of Beinsa Douno and developed and presented in an exceptionally clear, accessible and simple language (unlike the language of the Master Peter Deunov, which is characterized by immense mystic depth and multiple levels). At the same time, the methodology applied by Mihail Ivanov is a literal copy of some of the Master Peter Deunov's practices: meeting the sunrise, practicing Paneurhythmy, brotherly meals, singing spiritual songs, intense work according to the Master's praying practice, education in brotherly mutual help, etc.

Taking the foregoing into consideration, one can draw a conclusion through another sign concerning the Maitreya Bodhisattva given by Rudolf Steiner. It is known that after the radical transformation of the consciousness of the human bearer, he will appear spiritually powerful but as if alone in the world,[59] unrelated to any chain of Master-Disciple relationship. Therefore Mihail Ivanov cannot be the 20th century Bodhisattva because he has a spiritual Master, as he himself declares expressly. No one acquainted to any extent with the activity of this spiritual leader can make the mistake of asserting that he is the Bodhisattva described by spiritual science. This kind of error could have been avoided had thorough and impartial research into the matter been used as the basis for drawing a conclusion. The bases for rejecting the identifications of Valentine Tomberg and Mihail Ivanov are fundamentally different. In the life of Valentin Tomberg, there was a conspicuous rupture with the ideas he had previously embraced, connecting with completely different ideals of social impulses, the rejection of fundamental ideas of Anthroposophy, and eventually a clear underestimation of the significance and seriousness of the impulse given by Rudolf Steiner. In contrast, Mihail Ivanov identifies himself as a disciple of the Master Peter Deunov without interruption from his eighteenth year until the end of his life.

In order to discover the Grail, attention should be paid to the smallest things, but underpinned by sacred attitude, intelligently and free of criticism.

(6) When a human being develops its 'I'-aspect and aspires at the same time to a spiritual ideal, a typical

mistake can occur that is one of the pitfalls along the path of spiritual development. When a spiritually seeking 'I' intensively aspires to reach and emulate an elevated Master, a wellspring of Divine Wisdom, one sometimes falls into the error of self-identification with the object of his aspiration. There is within such a human ego a dangerous combination of a strong aspiration to a certain elevated objective and a latent vanity and megalomania: a mistaken identification of the disciple with the Master is the result. This destructive combination leads to a situation when followers of some esoteric paths who are familiar with prophecies about the new manifestation of the Maitreya Bodhisattva in the present epoch lose their grasp of themselves and on reality to such an extent that they actually want to proclaim themselves to the world as the manifestation of the World Great Master long-awaited by esotericists from the East and from the West. Often such a pseudo-esotericist makes unambiguous hints that he himself is the Maitreya Bodhisattva or, more usually, announces publicly about his 33rd year that he is no longer the old personality but is the Bodhisattva himself.

Rudolf Steiner, in order to protect any genuinely seeking follower of Esoteric Christianity from similar temptations, describes the esoteric principle that the Maitreya Bodhisattva, manifesting himself in 20th century, shall not proclaim himself.[60] This is done not only to comply with the laws of purity and humility in the esoteric path. If the Maitreya Bodhisattva were to declare openly who he is, he would sever the free conditions of the spiritual growth of contemporary esoteric disciples, which shall be fostered by their striving and the Grail-like aspiration to the Word of the Messenger of the Holy Spirit on the Earth as promised by Christ. The Bodhisattva, the greatest Master of the living power of the Christ who will one day become the first Buddha after the Mystery of Golgotha, will not announce his being and manifestation to the world. His divine individuality will work intensively for the Etheric Reappearance of the Christ within human souls; this is the most substantial, the most significant goal of the Maitreya Bodhisattva. Whether the human beings listening to his teaching and lectures will be developed enough to understand him clearly and to come to know him deeply or whether this happens after he completes his particular physical manifestation in the 20th century is a secondary matter directly related to the present level of development of humanity and to the presence of souls sufficiently advanced in spiritual science. It is as if the Masters of the White Lodge, through the prophesies about the Maitreya Bodhisattva which are accessible to everyone, put to the test the spiritual maturity and developmental level of the virtues of any esotericist working with this question. It should be remembered that the dark adepts, for their part, fill every vacuum of knowledge with all kinds of ungrounded speculation concealing its essence behind the drama of ceremonial esotericism and take advantage of people's ignorance and laziness towards research. Also relevant is the indication given by Rudolf Steiner that a period of a hundred years often elapses between the lifetime of a spiritual Master and widespread acquaintance with his identity and teaching. This is because at the present level of moral maturity of most of humanity, a widespread knowledge of the Master could result in harm both to him and to his followers.[61]

None of these characteristics and indications in esoteric science prevents the appearance of whatever pseudo-esotericists of megalomaniacal aspirations who directly and overtly proclaim themselves to the world as being the very Maitreya Bodhisattva himself who is prophesied to manifest both in Buddhist prophesies and in the works of Helena Blavatsky and Rudolf Steiner. For instance, L. Ron Hubbard (1911-1986), the founder of Scientology, wrote a poem around 1955 or 1956 entitled *Hymn of Asia* in which he unambiguously points to the prophesy of the Maitreya Bodhisattva being realized in his own person.[62]

A similar example is the activity of the founder of a religion in China. Lu Zhong Yi (1849-1925), the 17th patriarch of the spiritual movement of I-Kuan Tao, proclaimed himself the reincarnation of the Maitreya Bodhisattva.

A less complex situation is that of Benjamin Crème, an artist and esotericist born in Scotland in 1922 who founded the *Share International* organization. Having seen that the esoteric research on the topic of the Maitreya Bodhisattva was in a particular crisis, Benjamin Crème disregarded the 100-year rhythm of the manifestation of the Great Master as described by Rudolf Steiner.[63] He started talking, in 1975, about the idea that the Maitreya, long awaited by many, is on the Earth and manifested in various places on the planet. Benjamin Crème even exhibited a supposed picture of the Maitreya taken at a moment of his manifestation. This photograph was made during the so-called "case" in Kenya in 1988, when a man proclaiming himself the Maitreya appeared before six thousand people in Africa. Benjamin Crème started preparing a set of predictions and prognoses of where and when exactly the Master Maitreya will reappear; his prognoses were either ill-fabricated insinuations or theatrical performances or did not take place at all.

An even more eloquent and enlightening example is the life of Victor Manuel Gomez Rodrigez (1917-1977), born in South America (Bogota, Columbia), better known by the name of Samael Aun Weor. He had a difficult youth during which he not only suffered extreme poverty, wandering among the tribes in the Americas and being taken to prison several times, but also delivered lectures to a Theosophical audience and became profoundly acquainted with texts of the occult society *F.R.A.* (*Fraternitas Rosicruciana Antiqua*), including the works of Helena Blavatsky and Rudolf Steiner that were available in Central America at the time. He spoke openly about so-called *white sexual magic*. In 1960, during his 33rd year, he published *The Aquarian Message*, the introduction to which he signs: *Samael Aun Weor, Maitreya Buddha, Kalki Avatar of the New Age of Aquarius*, and states: *The Maitreya Buddha Samael is the Kalki Avatar of the New Age, he is the one who sat upon the white horse*, referring to the *White Rider* described in the Apocalypse of St. John. He also proclaimed himself for the predicted Great Master spoken about by spiritual leaders in the persons of Rudolf Steiner and Helena Blavatsky. Later on, he founded the *Gnostic Association for Anthropological, Cultural and Scientific Research* and came into contact with Swami Sivananda from India. He died of stomach cancer in the summer of 1977. It seems, however, that Samael Aun Weor had no access to Rudolf Steiner's lecture delivered on 21 September 1911 and did not understand that the Bodhisattva of the Good, the Bodhisattva of Virtue, is a wellspring of infinite humility and moral purity.

The one seeking the Holy Grail must be free of any vainglory and megalomania; he always remembers that he is just a humble traveler in the Path of Christ. This is the only way to continue ahead to the sacred aim.

(7) Every time the Grail challenges humanity to seek and find it, grave hardships are followed by a time of final trials related to the challenge, trials showing by their appearance that the Grail will soon be found. There are four kinds of final trials:

(i) the abandonment of hope in the desperation that comes from the deepest darkness, shortly before the first rays of dawn. Seekers either perish along the path, forget about seeking, or completely lose faith because of the grave hardships and reject the very existence of the Grail;

(ii) extreme difficulty in distinguishing between the true and the false. A few seekers of the Grail find the sacred mysterious place where the Holy Chalice is kept but find that it is hidden among numerous false multi-colored and dangerous cups, each one asking insistently to be chosen. Seekers stop breathing in fear and find it impossible to tell which cup is the true Grail;

(iii) the embracing of a false grail: some seekers sink into the enchantment of the hypnotic allure of some of the false chalices and thereby destroy themselves;

(iv) resignation from seeking the Grail and contentment with a description of the path of seeking. Such resignation gives rise to the feeling that *if we cannot know which among all the possible Grail cups the true Grail cup is, then the Grail cannot be found, now or ever, except in the higher worlds; and we shall have therefore to content ourselves with the enlightening words of the one who was pointing the path to the Grail.*

At the turn of the last century, Rudolf Steiner gathered noble, seeking souls and gave them clear indications about how to undertake a quest similar to finding the Holy Grail in our time, the Word of the Maitreya Bodhisattva as it manifested in the 20th century. Today, a hundred years later, some Anthroposophists feel discouraged and have given up seeking the Bodhisattva and his Word, maintaining that this search has no substance in or significance for the present time, is not worth the while pursuing, and therefore should not be a priority for Anthroposophists. Others, submerged in the trial that has been created by the proliferation of the many different hypotheses about who is the Bodhisattva, are paralyzed and sink into a bog of fear and doubt. Still others are enchanted with the false hypotheses already mentioned, and during their entire lives plant illusions and fallacies into other human souls.

A fourth group, represented by S. Prokofieff, argue that the Bodhisattva did not incorporate at all in the manner expected, but rather completed his mission through inspiration only. Prokofieff writes: *After the true task of the bodhisattva had been completely blocked by the leaders of the Theosophical Society at the time* [Annie Besant and Charles Leadbeater, through the proclamation of Krishnamurti as both the Christ and the Maitreya], *another human being had to help him fulfill it. Such a helper could only be an initiate who was incarnated on the earth at the same time, who firstly knew from his own experience about the mystery of the bodhisattvas...and secondly knew, again from his own experience, about the mystery of the etheric Second Coming of the Christ.... Such an initiate was Rudolf Steiner.... Hence the Maitreya Bodhisattva was able to fulfill his essential task through him. In this case the earthly personality of Rudolf Steiner was not, so to speak, taken hold of "from above"... but Rudolf Steiner consciously gave the bodhisattva the possibility of fulfilling his mission through him without any exchange of personality or a sudden transformation of his being...taking place.... [This] was possible as a result of the Rosicrucian initiation that Rudolf Steiner had received.*[64]

While considering these interesting suggestions and the reasoning underlying them, one can see how they contradict, both conceptually and logically, a number of statements made on this matter by Rudolf Steiner out of his initiate consciousness. We lay the greatest emphasis on four of them:

(i) *The Maitreya Bodhisattva...who was then, a hundred years before Christ, incarnated as Jeshua ben Pandira as the herald of the Christ in the physical body... he, who since then has incorporated once every hundred years, is incorporated now and will be the actual herald of Christ in etheric raiment...*[65]

(ii) Rudolf Steiner's statement in August 1921 with relation to the birth of the Bodhisattva at about the beginning of the century;[66]

(iii) *Also in our time* [the 20th century] *the most significant teachings about the Christ Being and the Sons of Fire of ancient India, the Agnishvattas, will come from that one who will once—not now, but in a future time—become the Maitreya Buddha...*[67]

(iv) *Every Bodhisattva who rises to Buddha has a successor. This oriental tradition fully corresponds to occult research. And that Bodhisattva, who worked then* [a hundred years before Christ] *for the preparation of the Christ Event, has incorporated again and again. One of these incorporations is to fall within the twentieth century.*[68]

Anyone regarding this contradiction as a genuine expression of the results of spiritual science who does not have a previous acquaintance with the work of Rudolf Steiner and an initial modest esoteric preparation can easily find himself seriously doubting the spiritual power of Rudolf Steiner and the veracity of Anthroposophy. In order to avoid a similar situation, let review the possible alternatives regarding the lack of agreement between the suggestions of later anthroposophical researchers we have examined, for instance Prokofieff and Lazaridès as well as other similar authors, and the statements of Rudolf Steiner. Regardless of how dangerous some of these alternatives may appear, a sober review will point up what is false and unreasonable, leaving only what is true and sensible. So, in the view of the authors of the present book, the possible alternatives are as follows:

(i) Rudolf Steiner was confused for a certain period of time and speaks inadequately and contradictorily about the entire structure of the Spiritual Science already expressed, and consequently there is need to correct him by other spiritual researchers;

(ii) Rudolf Steiner, in talking about the Maitreya Bodhisattva, his great mission in the future, and his present preaching about the Etheric Christ, does not properly assess the attacks of the dark powers and finds himself in the dangerously vainglorious situation of speaking, from an occult point of view non-hygienically, about a present Bodhisattva but having in fact himself in mind;

(iii) Rudolf Steiner, in speaking about the incorporation of the Maitreya Bodhisattva in the 20th century and about his task of being the true preacher of Christ in Etheric raiment, simply makes false statements which naturally then have no further effect, as was the case with Annie Besant, Elena Roerich, Alice Bailey, etc.

These three alternatives are available to us if we assume that the contemporary anthroposophical authors of the suggestions quoted above are right and that the founder of Anthroposophical Society somehow went astray.

(iv) However, if we assume the opposite, i.e. that Rudolf Steiner, being one of the great initiates of our time, is right, and the suggestions of some of his followers quoted above are conceptually wrong, we are left with the sole possibility that we are to take Rudolf Steiner's words literally, and that he describes precisely the actual event of the Bodhisattva of our time appearing physically in a human bearer in the 20th century and preaching the Etheric Appearance of Christ. At the same time, independent of the attacks of the dark powers on the truth in the form of false proclamations, Rudolf Steiner himself (under the inspiring influence of this Bodhisattva and due to his personal esoteric power) also offers the truth about the new appearance of the Christ Spirit. Thus two avenues for the Annunciation are ensured in our times. It is the view of the authors of this work that the propositions that Rudolf Steiner, an initiate, speaks in contradictions, are unconditionally untrue and categorically nonsensical, and anybody who takes up Anthroposophy in an open and unprejudiced way and approaches the matter with pure thought and a mindful heart, enlightened by the Christ ideal, will arrive at the same result.

Thus we come to the conclusion that only the fourth out of all examined alternatives has reasonable grounds. But then there arise questions regarding the impulses leading to the situation in which suggestions contradicting Rudolf Steiner are being put forward by later anthroposophical researchers. Without any intention of personal criticism or recrimination, we arrive at the idea that this situation has been reached because of the grave obstacles to implementing the Grail task implicitly assigned by Rudolf Steiner that arose for reasons that we can surmise. Foremost among these reasons, as the lengthy research efforts of many Anthroposophical leaders did not yield any results, is the supposition that the Bodhisattva did not incorporate and did not appear physically as a preacher of the Etheric Appearance in the 20th century but remained in the spiritual world. It is further supposed that he has been influencing Rudolf Steiner from there and thus was able to accomplish his mission solely through Rudolf Steiner because the dark powers in the early 20th century and their machinations were too strong. In other words: leading researchers within the Anthroposophical Society and Movement have concluded that success in the Grail-like search for the true preaching of the Etheric Appearance of the Christ, as Rudolf Steiner predicted would be given by the physically embodied Maitreya Bodhisattva in the 20th century, is not possible or no longer desirable. Thus, even at the price of obvious logical contradiction and doubt in the spiritual-scientific coherence of Rudolf Steiner's work, a tragic attempt has been made to create a self-contained conceptual entirety out of Anthroposophy, as if saying *we could not solve the problem assigned to us by our Master, and therefore he must have been wrong in the formulation of the problem; but at least we can hold on to what he taught us* – without seeing that, in saying this, what Rudolf Steiner taught has indeed been lost.

This error is founded on the assumption that the dark powers were so strong that they could stop the mission of a Bodhisattva. We are bound to ask: If it is assumed by the above researchers that the dark powers are so strong that they could stop the mission of the Bodhisattva, then should we not also assume that the bright light of the Holy Spirit, which is an aura and internal essence of the Herald of the Lodge of the Great Masters of Wisdom, is significantly much more powerful than all the machinations, taken together, of the mediumistic intermediaries of the pseudo-mahatmas? It is a fundamental principle that evil has its strength in quantity, while the good finds it strength in quality, that is: to many dark deeds of the adepts of evil, the Masters of the Christ Light can oppose one or two impulses, and this will be sufficient to balance adequately the dark powers or even be sufficient for their complete liquidation.

We must emphasize the fact that the position we have described and taken by certain serious anthroposophical researchers conceals another significant problem. Every century, the Bodhisattva who will one day become the Maitreya Buddha appears once again, including in the 20th century, as Rudolf Steiner predicted and as in fact occurred. If, however, anthroposophical researchers conclude the contrary, whether explicitly or by implication, that the Maitreya did not appear in the 20th century, then his life and teaching will not be researched, understood, or acknowledged, not only in anthroposophical circles but in humanity in general. This is because the social environment of the Anthroposophical Movement is, as such, a special spiritual organ of humanity. If, to our great misfortune, the 20th century appearance of the Bodhisattva were overlooked, then his subsequent appearances in the 21st and 22nd centuries will likely not be recognized properly by humanity, and people will hardly be able to have the right preparation for the culmination of the Maitreya's mission approximately 3000 years from now. Rudolf Steiner pointed out that it is critically important not only that humanity is normally developed in about 3000 years and aware of the Wisdom of the *Eightfold Path*, but, apart from this, that there is a need for people who throughout the centuries can properly recognize and realize in their own lives the commandments of the Bodhisattva and other Masters acting in Christ. This will transform the teaching of the Eightfold Path into the actual working power of Love streaming out of their souls into the whole world.[69] The Bodhisattva who will become Buddha Maitreya will need precisely such souls, matured in Love, to fully realize his mission.

Moreover, if we do not have a true and accurate understanding of the 20th century Bodhisattva, we shall not, in fact, have the correct preparation and adequate experience of the most significant event of the present Michael epoch, the Second, Etheric Appearance of Christ. This is the reason that Adolf Arenson, quoting Rudolf Steiner in lectures given in 1930, emphasized: *Only when we are oriented by the Bodhisattvas can we rise in a proper way to the understanding of what Christ was to humanity, what He can be and will constantly be in the future.*[70] Arenson, one of the first researchers into the Bodhisattva question who introduced an early version of the above-mentioned conclusions in the Anthroposophical Society, says explicitly that *we can be raised to a true knowledge of the deed of Christ only when we allowed first the Bodhisattva to orient us. This is nothing less than meaning that if we do not know the herald of Christ in 20th century, there will be a danger for us not to know Christ himself, when He appears in etheric raiment.*[71] Therefore it is critical to the whole development of contemporary esoteric Christianity not only to receive the inspiring manifestation of the Bodhisattva through Rudolf Steiner but to arrive at the end of the quest for the Bodhisattva and to find the specific, historically manifested teaching of the Maitreya Bodhisattva given for the sake of the Second Appearance of the Christ, rather than making a pronouncement, based on incomplete evidence and faulty reasoning, that the corporeal manifestation of the Bodhisattva did not occur.

The seeker of the Grail does not give up; he is a devoted seeker to the very end. He completes all the assigned tasks without doubting his Master and advances dauntlessly along the path without fear and darkness but in Love and Light!

Precisely this most difficult time, full of trials, constitutes a sign that the Dawning of the Holy Grail nowadays is close at hand. Let there be Light! In the name of the Dawn of the Master who contemplates directly the Christ Power and Life, let us free ourselves of all tempting hypotheses and take the decisive jump to the truth about the 20th century Bodhisattva.

A new thesis about the historical manifestation of the Maitreya Bodhisattva in the 20th century

In the next part of our study, we shall offer a new thesis concerning the personality in which the Bodhisattva appeared in 20th century and, most importantly, where we can find the contemporary written and spoken word of that Master whose task it is to bring the most profound understanding of Christ's mission. To begin with, however, we will make certain clarifications.

One of the major motives behind the present study is the intention to use spiritual-scientific methodology. According to the authors of this study, spiritual science is a specific synthesis of the characteristics of the ideals of contemporary scientific discourse.

On one hand are the elements of any science:

(i)   objectivity and freedom from any dogma;

(ii) readiness to consider any new, well-founded point of view;

(iii) systematic approach to clearly structured considerations and arguments; and

(iv) intellectual honesty and openness in the research process.

On the other hand are the characteristic features of spiritual research:

(i)   working with the internal processes and experiences of the consciousness of the researcher;

(ii) directing thought towards a transcendent spiritual reality;

(iii) navigating the complex environment of imaginative enlightenment, inspirative reflection and creative intuitive experiences;

(iv) continual vigilance regarding anything that tempts or blurs consciousness; and

(v)   a self-aware and resolute effort towards self-control over the newly received information from the internal processes based on virtuous self-verification.*

---

* This is an essential spiritual process that we find difficult to describe within the limits of the present work.

Having made these comments about methodology, we feel obligated to make these preliminary statements:

(i)   the debate of a new thesis is not aimed at introducing even greater chaos into the spiritual research on this topic and does not represent an attack against a new potential appearance of the Bodhisattva in the 21st century;

(ii) there is no *secret lodge* or *Jesuit order* commissioning the present research of ideas in this study;

(iii) if clear and well-founded evidence or reference sources are already available or are discovered that disprove the new thesis, the authors will fairly and openly revise it and will subject it to a thorough reconstruction or even retract it publicly because this study is, after all, only spiritual-scientific research of the Truth on the question of the Bodhisattva of the 20th century. Moreover, the research team is not obsessed with or attached to their theses;

(iv) the authors of this work have no personal opinion regarding the people who developed and produced any of the seven hypotheses mentioned and have made every effort to be impartial and remain

free of any fundamentalism or dogmatic
approach;

(v)   the authors are absolutely aware of the
serious responsibility involved in the
research and presentation of this thesis but
at the same time firmly believe that the
spiritual-scientific   approach   requires
Michaelic daring;

(vi)   the team developing these ideas is not
willing   to   impose   their   findings
fanatically.   Their ideals are freedom,
dedication to Michael, pure creative
thought   and   a   spiritual-scientific
approach.

Before we move to the essence of our new thesis,
we have to pay special attention to one important detail
of the last, seventh, hypothesis concerning the particular
appearance of the Bodhisattva.

As was already mentioned, Adolf Arenson, as early
as 1930, gave lectures putting forth an early form of this
hypothesis, and later on Sergei Prokofieff developed in
detail the same suggestion that in fact there was no
physical appearance of the Bodhisattva in 20th century
but only his spiritual influence, through inspiration, upon
Rudolf Steiner. It has already been shown that this idea
was burdened with a serious logical contradiction and
indicates a conceptual gap in the research of some
Anthroposophical leaders. On the one hand, we do not

agree with this hypothesis that at one point had substantial dissemination within official Anthroposophical circles, and we believe in the spiritual-scientific comprehensiveness of all the ideas, resting on logic throughout, put forward by Rudolf Steiner. On the other hand, we genuinely respect the considerable contribution of Sergei Prokofieff and we appreciate the path of research that he developed regarding the present topic. We believe that he approached this issue from honest spiritual-scientific positions and we are of the view that significant social and historical considerations have brought about such a hypothesis laden with internal contradictions.

It may be observed that the numerous unsuccessful attempts to find a spiritual impulse different in its creative feeling from the spiritual-scientific approach of Anthroposophy may be exhausting and lead to serious crises in renovation and a lack of consolidation within the social organism of the Anthroposophical Society. The ongoing conceptual battles over false and destructive hypotheses may bring about fatigue and disillusionment. Another important point is that Eastern Europe has been in political and cultural isolation for a very long time. There is a sort of information blockage resulting from the ideological causes of the so-called Cold War. This also slowed down the spiritual-scientific process and intensified the crisis of not finding the Bodhisattva. This weariness and slowing down, this spiritual-scientific crisis can be seen to have provoked a drive towards centralization as a means of protection against destructive tendencies. This impulse, however, carries a good deal of danger within itself. It is entirely possible to open the way to fundamentalism within the Anthroposophical Society through abandoning the pursuit of the other structural pole of contemporary Esoteric Christianity. Only when the cognitive clarity of spiritual science joins the moral impulse of the 20th century Bodhisattva will both realize their fullest potential. The Anthroposophical Society may then gradually come into the danger of losing the *scientific* aspect of its spiritual-scientific research and transforming into a stereotypical religious organization. The increased centralization of the Society since the 1950s may amplify this development through the natural tendency of a strongly centralized organization away from independent research that fosters a multitude of perspectives. Therefore, an impulse of renewal that Anthroposophy will acquire in the event that the truth about the 20th century Bodhisattva is revealed and access to his Word provided may prove significant and indispensable for the realization of Spiritual Science in its entire Michaelic ideal.

The spiritual-historical demand placed before humanity through the Will of the Cosmic Being of the Christ, the Will of all the Christ Hierarchies, and the Will of the Great Masters of humanity gathered at the spiritual council in the 4th century A.D. inspired and brought about the unification of the two branches of the True Christianity, the Western one manifested by Rudolf Steiner and inspired by spiritual giants like Christian Rosenkreutz and the Master Jesus, and the Eastern of the Maitreya Bodhisattva as manifested in 20th century. The latter is one who took over the tiara of the Holy Spirit from the Gautama Buddha and appeared in the Essenian Master Jeshu ben Pandira, who by his sacrifice opened the way for the descent of Christ onto the Earth.

It has already been mentioned that due to several occult, ethical, and social reasons, Rudolf Steiner could not directly point to the person through whom the Maitreya Bodhisattva appeared.[72] What are these reasons more specifically? Rudolf Steiner, being a true spiritual leader, worked on a large scale in almost all of Central and Western Europe. In these circumstances, he hinted that during his time there was another Master, physically manifested, of a very high level. Although Rudolf Steiner, judging by the comments made in his lectures, is clearly in continual contact with this Master, he cannot directly name the person because this would have presented an enormous temptation for those unprepared souls. It is very easy to reach a disastrous situation for Anthroposophy where hundreds of *pilgrims* (following a direct announcement) could rush to the new Messenger of God, and this would actually be a violation of the esoteric laws in life. The true spiritual leaders of humankind, who are purely humble Disciples of Christ, have always protected themselves and their associates from inappropriate adoration. To avoid this, it generally takes about a hundred years before people can rightly understand and appreciate any given spiritual impulse. Rudolf Steiner takes this rhythm into consideration and foreseeing the appearance of another spiritual leader during the first half of 20th century, he did his best to protect himself, his followers, and also the foreseen spiritual leader and his potential followers from the venom of pride and inopportune adoration. Indeed, Rudolf Steiner, with Michaelic wisdom, created the conditions of freedom for a spiritual-scientific, Grail-like seeking and esoteric Christian mystical development for all those who accepted the challenge of his legacy and took up the search for the 20th century Bodhisattva.

So we can move now to an in-depth discussion of our new thesis. To begin with, let us recall what is probably one of the most important indications given us by Rudolf Steiner (November 4, 1911): *the Maitreya Bodhisattva... is also incorporated now, and will be the actual herald of the Christ in etheric raiment.* We maintain that Rudolf Steiner, in articulating these words, did not simply have full earthly consciousness but also the cosmically expanded consciousness of a genuine initiate who encompasses with his awareness the entire development of humanity. Moreover, we hold that he spoke truly and clearly when he said that the name of *Maitreya Bodhisattva* did not refer to his own personality. In other words, Rudolf Steiner did, in fact, state clearly that there is another Messenger of Christ, appearing in parallel with him during the first several decades of 20th century, generating a powerful esoteric Christian impulse in the service of the Etheric Appearance of the Christ.

Taking this statement as a point of departure for our thesis, we shall try first to apply formal logic, meta-analysis[73] of existing studies, and reflection through the contemporary scientific methods applied in the investigation of a certain cultural process through historical and geographical methods. If we are to look for a particular teaching, understandable to any human being and delivered by a Messenger of the Etheric Appearance of Christ other than Rudolf Steiner, we would be mistaken to imagine that this historical appearance manifested in a non-Christian cultural environment or in an environment of relative cultural isolation remote from the main center of development of the contemporary cultural epoch: Europe. In other words, if we are to find a widely known historical event of a spiritual nature related to the very center of Christianity, we should hardly begin by looking for it in the jungles of Africa or in the deserts of Asia where Christianity is poorly represented among the local cultures. We should hardly be looking for it in the yet young cultural situation on the South American continent, which is still rather dependent on the European spiritual culture and does not actively manifest self-generated impulses in the strict spiritual-scientific sense of contemporary esoteric Christianity. On the other hand, during the period under review, numerous Christian movements existed in the North American continent: Mormons, Quakers, Methodists, the followers of Elena Vite, and so on. These are predominantly spiritual movements derived from Protestantism. Although some of them become rather influential, they share a feature that disqualifies them from a potential link with the Maitreya Bodhisattva. That feature is the fact that all of them either do not seek the Second Appearance of Christ in 20th century at all or they seek it on the physical plane.

So we arrive at two conclusions, one regarding the time of the appearance of the Maitreya Bodhisattva in the 20th century, the second regarding the place.

The first is that we should look for him in the early decades of the century, before the horrors of the Second World War. This follows from the words quoted above to the effect that the Maitreya was incorporated in 1911, as well as Rudolf Steiner's statement in August 1921 putting the birth of the Bodhisattva (not the human bearer) at about the beginning of the century. Together, they indicate that the incorporation of the Maitreya Bodhisattva into a human bearer had to have taken place before 1911, most probably within five years of the turn of the century, in the period 1895-1905. As the radical change manifested by the human bearer in the spiritual texture of his consciousness took place when he was 30-

35 years of age, the birth of the human bearer would have fallen in the range of years 1860-1875.

In this respect, we are in substantial disagreement with certain research work exhibiting materialistic inclinations not following the tenets of the Spiritual Science. Those undertaking such research believe they have to locate a physical birth of a person at the beginning of the 20th century and who would therefore be at age 33 in 1933. It is our belief to the contrary that one should look, as we have stated above, for a person born in the period 1860-1875 and incorporated by the Bodhisattva around the turn of the century at 30-35 years of age, and that there begins then a powerful spiritual-moral activity in parallel with the victory of the Archangel Michael and the end of the Kali Yuga. In the significant period of 1933-1936-1939, he would therefore have been 58-79 years old.

The second conclusion regards the place of the appearance of the Bodhisattva. If we accept the idea that the Maitreya was active at the same time that Rudolf Steiner was, we shall reach the conclusion that, during the intensive lecturing work of Rudolf Steiner in Western and Central Europe, there must have already been another powerful esoteric Christian impulse, also in Europe. We can also infer from that lack of comment by Rudolf Steiner on the subject that that impulse did not appear in the part of Europe in which Rudolf Steiner was active. If it had, we can well suppose that Rudolf Steiner would have commented specifically on this, as he had done with other spiritual impulses manifested in this part of Europe. In other words, we have to look somewhere in Eastern Europe for the impulse of the Bodhisattva. This conclusion is consonant with two important considerations: first, the Bodhisattva himself manifests eastern Christian wisdom and a spiritual brotherly way of life (particularly bearing in mind his Essenian historical manifestation). Second, Eastern Europe with its Black Sea coast is a highly favorable environment for a powerful spiritual manifestation. In the 7th-8th centuries A.D., for instance, the Gautama Buddha centered his work from the spiritual world in the esoteric schools manifested physically in the area of the Black Sea coast.[74] Apart from this, we might well expect that the Bodhisattva would appear among the Slavic folk in order to ennoble and prepare these people because he will become the Maitreya Buddha around the culmination of the sixth, the Slavic, cultural epoch. In this way, we have considerably narrowed the geographical range of the cultural manifestation of the esoteric Christian impulse of the Bodhisattva.

Let us bring forth another argument through the method of formal logic, an argument that can produce a substantial result relevant to our study. If we take as given that there was a personality who was the bearer of the Maitreya Bodhisattva at the beginning of 20th century, this means that he gave a great teaching aimed at imparting a profound understanding of Christ's mission on the Earth. If Rudolf Steiner, the great initiate of true Rosicrucianism, left humanity over three hundred volumes (several thousand of lectures), studies of immense spiritual depth and power, as well as numerous practical and spiritual-social forms, then let us imagine what an abundance of divine benediction must have been brought by the one whom Rudolf Steiner called the greatest Master of the impulse of Christ and who, in the 20th century, will be the greatest herald of Christ, of His Second Appearance in the Astral world in Etheric raiment. Thanks to this indication, we can find a real spiritual-scientific method for the discovery of the truth about the Bodhisattva in our time. Thus we reach the conclusion that if we have to look for the Word and the Teaching of the 20th century Bodhisattva, we will not find it expressed in substandard lecturing, a few books and insufficient spiritual methodology. We shall find it, rather, taken up across a wide social strata, and featuring a lecturing so intense that it is considered preaching about the immediate activity of the Spirit of Christ. We shall find it contained in hundreds of volumes (several thousand of lectures) and rooted in esoteric Christian methodology, based on spiritual traditions characteristic of ancient times and manifested through a brotherly way of life.

So, taking this as a point of departure, we can move on and put forward other simple questions: how many different spiritual denominations were there in Europe during the first half of 20th century; which ones are they and what typical features do they have? Do they have anything in common with Esoteric Christianity? Do these spiritual denominations apply contemporary and suitable methodology, consistent with the required freedom and occult hygiene with respect to the present Epoch of the Consciousness Soul?

Undoubtedly, the Anthroposophical Society is, in principle, one of the most significant factors in human spiritual development, but for reasons already explained it is not possible to seek the physically manifested Bodhisattva in it. The Theosophical impulse, starting with Blavatsky and developed further by Leadbeater and Besant, uses mediumistic methods which conflict with the spiritual hygiene of contemporary, free people and has clearly nothing to do with real esoteric Christianity. In additional, the Theosophical impulse diametrically opposes the ideas expressed by Rudolf Steiner about the 20th century Bodhisattva through its proclamation of Krishnamurti as the Maitreya. The teachings of the Roerichs contained in Agni Yoga and the materials given by Alice Bailey are similar in that regard. The books of Papus and Eliphas Levi have nothing to do with the idea of the Bodhisattva. The so-called Rosicrucian impulse as it was founded by Max Heindel has other goals and objectives; it appears predominantly outside Europe and cannot be related to a Bodhisattva appearance.[75] The

Christian communities of the Duhobori and of the Tolstoyans in Russia, successors of the Hussites, the so-called Moravian Brothers spread also in Russia, the Netherlands and in America, together with the Quakers in England, take an active part in the spiritual life of Europe but cannot be related to the particular impulse of the Maitreya Bodhisattva, or at least there is no information corroborating the fact that a powerful spiritual leader appeared among them who was able to bring another preaching about the Second Appearance of the Christ. The life, activities and the materials given by Valentine Tomberg and Mihail Ivanov have already been discussed, and it was made clear that these two personalities do not meet the requirements connected with the appearance of the Bodhisattva. Evidently none of these spiritual movements manifests the teaching of the Bodhisattva.

On the other hand, if we examine the historical and cultural legacies of the countries in Eastern Europe during the first half of the 20th century for a new and powerful impulse based in esoteric Christianity, we shall not find this in Lithuania, in Latvia, or in Estonia, or in Poland or Romania. We have already commented on the situation in Russia and have pointed out that there are substantial spiritual impulses there, related to Christianity but which cannot be linked with the impulse of the Bodhisattva. After 1917, moreover, the spiritual environment in Russia changed drastically, and Russia became, beyond doubt, unsuitable for any esoteric impulse widely known in society. During the period under discussion, the Ukraine was at a special stage of historical development, but, leaving this aside, we once again cannot find the impulse we are looking for within its territory. The situation in the present-day countries of Serbia, Montenegro, Croatia, Macedonia and Bosnia and Herzegovina is similar. In Turkey, the social circumstance in terms of the development of a Christian teaching are utterly unfavorable, as evidenced, for example, by the genocidal massacre during this time of about one million Christian Armenians. Greece has the conditions for development of an esoteric Christian teaching across broad social ranges but there are no indications of any such teaching having appeared. This leaves one country only, a country bordering the Black Sea, having a Slavic population and Cyrillic alphabet, Christian cultural values and a very ancient spiritual tradition, the country of Bulgaria.

The western coast of the Black Sea was inhabited by a highly developed civilization of cultural significance to the whole of humanity and older than the Sumerian by thousands of years. In the territory of present-day Bulgaria, among the Thracian tribes, the Apollo Bodhisattva appeared through Orpheus. According to Herodotus, Zamolksis, a slave of Pythagoras, whom he set free, went back to his fatherland, most probably the delta of the Danube River along the northeastern coastline of Bulgaria, and founded a school similar to the school of Pythagoras. He preached a doctrine about life after death and about reincarnation.

The Black Sea area of the present day Bulgaria is indelibly permeated with the apostolic mission of the Apostle St. Andrew, who founded in the town of Odessos (the present-day city of Varna) an episcopal early Christian church perhaps already in the second half of 1st century A.D.[76] The activity of the Gautama Buddha during the 7th to 8th centuries in the spiritual field of the Black Sea most likely coincides with the establishment of Bulgaria, one of the earliest kingdoms in Europe, along the delta of the Danube in the early 7th century. The local tribes formed the foundation of contemporary Bulgarian ethnicity. These people adopted Christianity as their official religion, and in parallel with this they adopted and preserved the Slavic alphabet of Saints Cyril and Methodius, two of the patrons of contemporary Europe. Thus Bulgaria became a spiritual and cultural center for the Slavic people living in what came to be known later as Eastern Orthodox Christianity. It was exactly during the time of the First Bulgarian Kingdom when a renewed Manichaean teaching, Bogomilism, spread for the first time through Europe on a large scale. Bogomilism was developed by Boyan the Magus (Benjamin), the third son of Tsar Simeon the Great (by his second wife Mariam), with the assistance of two mysterious Syrian initiates who brought the originals of the Gospel of John to the esoteric Christian School that Boyan established. The doctrine of Divine Mercy spread broadly over the whole of Bulgaria. In this way, the spiritual impulse of the Great Master Manes made its first contact with the Slavic population.[77] Many communities were established on the principle of brotherhood that practiced values then unknown in Europe, such as the reformation of social and political structures, a brotherly way of life, spiritual freedom, gender equality, vegetarianism, and a determination to apply the principles of the original Christianity. Although they were persecuted and burnt at the stake, they managed to spread the spark of Reformation and Renaissance all over Europe through their direct spiritual successors, the Albigensians, the Burgers, the Cathars, and the Rosicrucians.[78]

Precisely in the places where these influential spiritual conditions were present,[79] where the Great Masters of humanity worked, including Orpheus, Pythagoras, Buddha, Manes, a strong esoteric Christian teaching appeared in Bulgaria in 20th century, established by the Master Peter Deunov. It was called, as has already been mentioned, *The Teaching of the Universal White Brotherhood* and has as its Head the Spirit of Christ, who guides a ten-level spiritual organism, from advanced human souls to the Spirits of Love, the Seraphim. This teaching, based in Christianity, renewed the principles of *karma* and *reincarnation*, and spread on a large scale throughout the entire territory of Bulgaria in the course of several decades.

Peter Deunov (1864-1944) was born near the Black Sea, in the city of Varna, where the White Brotherhood Synarchic Chain began. An annual Brotherhood Assembly was held at the heart of Bulgaria, in the medieval capital of Veliko Tarnovo. A Brotherhood community of hundreds of followers, called *Izgrev* (meaning *Sunrise*), was founded in the only capital in Europe bearing the sacred name of *Sophia*. From 1914 onwards, several hundred Sunday lectures on the esoteric understanding of the mission of Christ, referring to the Gospels, were held in Sofia. These lectures constitute the series of books titled *Power and Life*.[80] The first Christian esoteric school in Europe ran from 1922 to 1944, having two classes (Youth Class and General Class), each of which had 23 annual cycles. Unique methodology is applied on the basis of the spiritual traditions of esoteric Christianity: mystic work with the Word; meeting the sunrise; practicing physical exercises permeated with spiritual meaning; contemplating the mystic imaginative picture in the form of a *Pentagram* depicting the steps of the path of the disciple; singing spiritual songs and systematic work with mystic music; intensive work through praying; reflection and meditation upon specially selected texts from the Bible, based on the assignment of colors given in the Master's book *The Testament of the Color Rays of Light;* practicing vegetarianism and fruit eating; fasting devoted to ideal striving; practicing the mystery of common brotherly meals; daily education in brotherly assistance and love to everything living. Some of the most impressive methods applied by the Master Peter Deunov are the Brotherhood Assemblies, excursions and outings to places of altitudes over 2000 meters for the purpose of inner development, through which sacred *love for living intelligent nature*, which is an expression of the creative work of the angelic hierarchies, was fostered. The culmination of the pure brotherly life of the thousands of followers of the Teaching is the experience of the presence of Christ through a live cosmogony in the form of synthesis of music, lyrics, mystic dance, visualized meditation, and prayer, a synthesis called *Paneurhythmy* that has its effect etherically. Master Peter Deunov stands out as an exceptionally good therapist: thousands of Bulgarians were healed through spiritual, natural, and non-traditional methods. As a sacred testament to humanity, the Master Peter Deunov left over four thousand lectures published in some three hundred volumes as well as several dozen musical works. Up to the present day, he is the most published author in Bulgaria. In 2006, he was listed in the top ten most popular Bulgarians in a national survey of the Bulgarian National TV. It is only natural that the tremendous activity of the Master Peter Deunov had tens of thousands of followers all over Bulgaria and resulted in the establishment of dozens of spiritual centers worldwide. Peter Deunov's spiritual name is Beinsa

Douno, coming from a proto-language, called Vatan by the Master. There is no definite translation, but researchers of this topic suggest it means: The one who conveys the Good though the Word.

Now it is time to bring together everything addressed so far.

During the time of Rudolf Steiner and for two decades afterwards in one Eastern European Slavic country a powerful esoteric Christian teaching appeared, developed by a prophet, healer, musician and above all a Master of Christ's power and life – the Master Peter Deunov. Indeed, during the first half of the 20th century there were two active true esoteric Christian schoolings in Europe: the Anthroposophy developed by Rudolf Steiner and the teaching of the Universal Brotherhood of Light, given by the Master Peter Deunov. Rudolf Steiner said: *Now in the 20th century, from this Bodhisattva come the most substantial teachings about the Christ Being and about the Sons of Fire... the Maitreya Bodhisattva is incorporated now as well and will be the actual herald of Christ in etheric raiment.*[81] As if to make Rudolf Steiner's word true, *that there will come a time... when the name of this Bodhisattva will be pronounced, who will rise to Maitreya Buddha*[82] we are now, a hundred years after the events that are the subject of this study, able to formulate our main thesis:

THESIS: Our conclusion is that when Rudolf Steiner spoke about the appearance of the Maitreya

Bodhisattva in the 20th century, he must have meant
the spiritual leader working in Bulgaria known under
the spiritual name of Beinsa Douno, called the *Master*
by his disciples, and appearing in the highly
developed personality of Peter Deunov.

Given that the logical approach to formulating the new thesis concerning the appearance of the Maitreya Bodhisattva in the 20th century has been relatively indirect, we shall now verify directly whether the main spiritual-scientific indications given by Rudolf Steiner correspond to the Word of the Master Peter Deunov and to some of the well-known facts and events of his life.

1. How does the Master Peter Deunov perceive and understand the Christ?

To provide a comprehensive answer to this question, it would be necessary to quote from and summarize thousands of lectures and speeches. The Master Peter Deunov spoke mainly about Divine Love, Wisdom, Truth, Justice, and Virtue as all stemming from the Christ Being. As it is not possible to quote at length within the limits of this text, we shall focus on several excerpts of the Word of the Master to introduce some of the basic ideas of this eastern branch of esoteric Christianity that was spread through the activities of the Master Beinsa Douno.

What is Christ?—Christ is a collective spirit. This is a sum of all the Sons of God, whose souls and hearts *pour forth Love and Life. All the Sons of God joined together, all the intelligent souls living in Divine unity, this is Christ. In this respect, He is the Head of the Great Universal Brotherhood.... And when we talk about the Great Universal Brotherhood, we understand the hierarchy of Intelligent Beings who have completed their evolution millions and billions of years before human beings and who now guide the entire Cosmos. According to the level of knowledge and development and according to the function they perform, these Beings are placed in a hierarchical ladder...: Seraphim, Cherubim, Thrones, Dominions, Mights, Powers, Archai, Archangels, Angels, and advanced human souls... All these taken together represent **the Great Cosmic Human Being.**[83]*

Christ is a divine cosmic being. A Divine Being that comes from the Central Sun of the Universe, around which our sun revolves and completes one revolution in twenty million year.[84] Christ comes from this Sun of the Universe. Christ is the greatest being.[85]

There is neither in the Cosmos outside, nor in the mystic depths of the soul inside, a greater manifestation of Love than that which we identify with Christ.... Today people divide Christ into 'historic', 'cosmic', 'mystic', etc. But Christ per se is One and Indivisible. There is only one Christ—the Living Christ, who is a manifestation of God, a manifestation of Love. Christ— this is God, Who discloses before the world.... And when

I talk about Christ, I consider Him not an abstract principle but a real incorporation of Love.[86]

2. Did the Master Peter Deunov speak in a special way about the Reappearance of the Christ in the etheric in the present epoch, as Rudolf Steiner predicted the 20th century Maitreya Bodhisattva would do?

We shall give merely some quotations regarding this matter:

There is no epoch in human history when Christ worked like this. Today, Christ works most of all. Several centuries ago, Christ was above, in the highest worlds, but now He has descended lower, into the astral and etheric worlds, closer to the material world. Two great events will take place: first, the Spirit of Christ will begin revealing itself in human beings; certainly, this will start with advanced souls. When you experience a fine, unselfish feeling, you experience compassion, love, mercy, and this indicates that the Spirit of Christ has dawned on you and starts working within. The Apostle Paul says too, 'It is no longer I who live, but Christ lives in me.'[87]

Christ will come, this is beyond doubt; and he will come soon.... The Second Appearance of the Christ should not be understood to mean the end of the world but the second coming of Christ.[88]

Christ is close to the physical level and he is present this year.... Christ is before us and among us, so I want you to open your hearts before Him. Entrust your soul to God and He will give to you as no one else can give to you. Throughout every year, we have to use the Name of God as Power and He will be our sentinel.... Christ is coming to reconcile humanity with the White Brotherhood of Light, the Brotherhood of Lights.[89]

I want you, above all, to have inner peace because we, during the present times, witness a great event that occurred on the Earth and that has been expected for thousands of years. Wise people, the prophets, spoke about it in ancient times; contemporary clairvoyants also speak about it, you have been expecting it, too. All have spoken about the coming of Christ and I shall not describe it to you because you will see it for yourselves.... You should not fear. Fear will divert your attention in the opposite direction, while Christ, Whom you address, carries with Him Divine Justice, Divine Love, Wisdom, Truth, which will enlighten the world and will bring it into order... During the epoch starting now, Christ will assign you a place to serve Him and you will be pleased to do the work He would assign to you.... The war taking place now is a war between the light and the dark sides of the astral world. This battle is going on in the dark side. And when you approach the boundary, you will see Christ.... Christ is now descending to us from the Divine World.... You still want to see Christ, but many of

*you have already seen Him, they have even seen Him
many times but they have almost always said, 'This may
not be Him, this may be someone else'.... Christ is here
and I would like you to keep your eyes open.*[90]

*3. Rudolf Steiner says expressly that the Maitreya
Bodhisattva shall not preach about a new physical
appearance of Christ, this being one of the most
significant characteristics by which we shall be able to
recognize the 20th century Bodhisattva. Does Master
Beinsa Douno preach about a second physical
incorporation of Christ or not?*

The Master Peter Deunov firmly denies any second
physical incorporation of Christ. We shall give one of the
many eloquent quotations on this matter:

*Christ works in the world but people do not see
him. They want to see Him as a human being, to touch
Him, to sense Him physically. If He fills the hearts of
people with beautiful and elevated feelings, what else
could you want? You want to caress Him, to kiss Him, to
carry Him in your hands? This is not an idea. What can
the child gain if you carry it in your arms all day long?
The people who expect Christ to be born again as a
young child are people with a wrong outlook. Christ was
born and keeps being born in the hearts and souls of
people. Nowadays, Christ cannot be borne by a woman.
If you expect the coming of the Redeemer, open your
souls, He will be born there. Moreover, Christ is being*

born simultaneously in many people. When Christ is born in your soul, you will be useful both to yourself and to the people around you. This is Resurrection. This is the awakening of the human soul. When Christ lives in people's souls, everyone will become alive, will rise and join hands like brothers.[91]

4. It is known from the indications given by Rudolf Steiner that the appearance of the Maitreya Bodhisattva shall not be known before the particular physical human-bearer reaches the age of 30 to 33. Did Peter Deunov manifest his social mission widely before the age of 30 to 33 or not? Is there any evidence of incorporation or a radical transformation of the consciousness of the human being called Peter Deunov? Did Peter Deunov have a physically present spiritual Master teaching him along a spiritual succession of Master and Disciple or did he, to the contrary, spread his teaching entirely on his own?

The issue of the transformation of the human being called Peter Deunov into the Master Beinsa Douno is one of the fundamental questions in the spiritual tradition of the White Brotherhood in Bulgaria. This question characterizes the very basis of this teaching and is simultaneously the key to the development of the human soul, a key to self-sacrifice, deep humility, and ineffable Love. Any serious researcher of esotericism in Bulgaria knows that a mystic sacrifice occurred in the consciousness of Peter Deunov when he was about 33 years old. This transformation of the personality of the progressively minded son of the Revivalist Deunov family took place in several stages, by penetrating and changing his life permanently. Until then, Peter Deunov sought solitude in order to work intensively upon himself; after the age of 33, however, he became involved in large-scale lecturing and spiritual organizational work having as an aim the spreading of a powerful esoteric impulse. Boyan Boev, one of the Master's closest disciples who attended many conversations of Beinsa Douno with his followers, gives this description:

The Master received a sister and told her:

'I am incorporated and this happened on 19 March 1897. I received a mission from heaven at that time. Then I was told that I was a Master to all humanity. The mission assigned to me is related to the new path of the Slavs and with the coming of the Sixth Epoch.'

It must be noted that the incorporation of the Master happened in several stages. The Master told me that when he was fasting and praying and climbed a mountain in the village of Arbanassi, near the town of Veliko Tarnovo, Christ appeared before him and told him, 'Surrender your body, your mind and your heart, and work for Me'. The Master responded, 'God, let Your Will be, I am ready!' (This happened... in the month of September 1914.)[92]

It is important to pay attention to the fact that, in March 1897, Peter Deunov is in his 33rd year, having been born on 11 July 1864. Apart from this, there is a well-established understanding among his followers (in relation to a number of speeches made by the Master Beinsa Douno and also with innumerable concrete experiences), that the personality of Peter Deunov and the personal course of life were sacrificed in the name of the *Master's Principle,* which was manifested as he reached the age of 33. From this point of view, when talking about Peter Deunov, we mean an advanced human personality who transformed into a unique Grail for the *Master's Principle,* and when we talk about the Master Peter Deunov or the Master Beinsa Douno, we in fact contemplate the deeds of the Master through the human being of Peter Deunov. Above all, it should be categorically stated that the Master Beinsa Douno is not a conductor of any spiritual tradition according to the accustomed way of physically manifested teaching along a *Master-Disciple* lineage. The words of Rudolf Steiner describe perfectly the situation: the Master Beinsa Douno appearing through Peter Deunov *will call upon... the power of his own word, and will stand as a human being alone in the world.*[93]

5. *If there are manifestations of rather dangerous and dark tendencies in various pseudo-spiritual teachings, identifying Christ with the anticipated*

Maitreya, what did the Master Peter Deunov say on this question? Does he identify himself with Christ?

This issue is not only dangerous and dark; it was created by demonic forces that want to undermine completely the activity of esoteric Christianity today. The tendency to identify Christ with the Maitreya is evident among Theosophical circles, and we have already commented on this matter. As was already mentioned, the Master Beinsa Douno worked specifically towards correcting the delusion of the Theosophical Society concerning the appearance of the World Master through Krishnamurti. The Master Peter Deunov sent a special messenger who, immediately before the moment of the organized announcement of Krishnamurti as World Master, handed him the Master's letter. The events are enlightening that were described in the memoirs of Atanas Dimitrov, a follower of the Master Peter Deunov who participated in the youth class of the Esoteric School and was a regular member of the Bulgarian Theosophical Society. Dimitrov attended the annual Theosophical meeting in the castle of Erde, in the Netherlands, in 1929. Before the Congress, he became a friend of Krishnamurti and often told him of the Master Peter Deunov, of his powerful Word and of the activity of the Spiritual School in Sofia. At the Congress, Krishnamurti denied that he was the World Master and Christ in the following words: *It is not I who am the World Master, it is not I who am Christ*, and Sophronii Nikov, the Head of the Bulgarian

Theosophical Society who also attended the Congress, remembers Krishnamurti also saying *The World Master is in Bulgaria.*[94]

It is only natural to put the question of what the attitude of the Master Peter Deunov was to the Theosophical Society. In the same memoirs the following situation is described, how the Theosophical representatives in Bulgaria saw that Peter Deunov, well known throughout society for his esoteric activity, was an excellent candidate to become a Theosophical worker and member. They invited him personally to join the Theosophical Society and promised an even wider popularity in Bulgaria and in the world. The Master Peter Deunov listened to them carefully and gave them a flat refusal, which shows once again the serious ideological differences between the teaching of the Universal White Brotherhood and Theosophy, then led by Annie Besant and Charles Leadbeater. The events described above, reported in memoirs, can be considered as one more piece of indirect evidence supporting our thesis. Actually only two physically manifested spiritual leaders worked against the popular delusion in Theosophical circles expressed in the announcement of Krishnamurti as the reincarnated Christ and Maitreya. These were Rudolf Steiner and Beinsa Douno.

The Master Peter Deunov is absolutely clear and firm on the issue of the physical appearance of Christ anticipated by these circles. Together with this he put a final end also to the mistaken attitude of certain of his followers towards him in the following mystic words:

Your attitude towards me is an attitude towards the White Brotherhood. And your attitude towards the White Brotherhood is your attitude towards God. You have to follow either Moses or Jesus or me, we are one. Moses' teaching is divine, as is Christ's divine teaching, as is mine. That Christ, Who was in Jesus, is the same Christ Who is in me, the Spirit is one. You have to implement one of these Teachings precisely in its full scope. I would like you to implement all three of them. God's Blessing will be measured according to the degree of your sincerity....

Do not seek for Christ on the physical level. Do not try to find Him in one person because He is in all people. Where Christ is manifested you will see an intense Light. Christ is One and many.

Sometimes you say: 'Is Mr. Deunov Christ, or is Christ within him?' I will tell you that I am not Christ, but Christ is in me.

If I were Christ, for Whom you take me, I would rule the whole world; as long as I am not such a person, I am not Christ either. Christ is not in the physical world.[95]

If we accept this new thesis about the appearance of the Bodhisattva in the 20th century and if we examine at length the words quoted above, we shall ascertain the accuracy of Rudolf Steiner's words, namely that the

Maitreya Bodhisattva shall not preach any second physical appearance of Christ. Moreover, the messenger of the Lodge of the Bodhisattvas shall not point at himself as the newly arrived Christ, and nobody should identify him with a new physical appearance of Christ. The Bodhisattva contemplates the Christ Being directly and is a sacred spring from which Christ's power and life stream. On the other hand, a person well acquainted with Anthroposophical ideas immediately notices the triple perspective in the above quotation: Moses' teaching, Christ's teaching, and the teaching of Beinsa Douno, which can be interpreted as a specific statement of the herald of the Holy Spirit on the Earth.

6. Is there any information about the specific perspective of Rudolf Steiner to the activity of Peter Deunov? What is the attitude of the Master Beinsa Douno to Rudolf Steiner?

It is known from certain statements of Rudolf Steiner's that there was a spiritual relationship between him and the Bodhisattva of the 20th century. In memoirs of some of the closest disciples of the Master Beinsa Douno there are certain additional details. It is interesting to see how Boyan Boev found his way to the teaching of Beinsa Douno. He is known as the person who was so close to the Master Peter Deunov that he was allowed to write down many of the personal conversations with his followers, and apart from that compiled some of the most significant books about the teaching of the Master (*The Master, The Wellspring of Good, Tuning of the Human Soul, etc.*). After the Master left the physical world, Boyan Boev took part in the organizational council of the White Brotherhood Society.

Boyan Boev was a student in natural sciences at university in Munich, and he once attended a course of Rudolf Steiner's lectures (Apocalypse, 1908, Nuremberg). In a personal conversation, of which memoirs and shorthand notes have survived, Steiner asked Boev where he came from. In response to the answer that he came from Bulgaria, Steiner told him that Bulgaria was a very important country and instructed him to go back and find the spiritual Master there. After this fateful conversation, Boyan Boev followed Steiner's advice and later became one of the most ardent followers of the Master Beinsa Douno. Since 1909 Boyan Boev maintain correspondence with Rudolf Steiner and Marie Steiner. Some of those letter are available in Rudolf Steiner's archive in Dornach. In December.1909 they communicate about searching for the Masters of Wisdom and July.1916 they avoid writing more about it due to privacy and sensitivity of information. Meanwhile in 1912, Boyan Boev has found the Master Peter Deunov. When the event in Nuremberg, how Boyan Boev found the Master Peter Deunov, was told to Pasha Todorova, one of the short-hand taking sisters, working on recording the Word of the Master Peter Deunov, she asked him: *You, Master, do you know Rudolf Steiner?* The Master responded: *'Of course, I know him.' 'Master, have you seen him here on the Earth?* The Master replied: *'Not here on Earth; above in Heavens, this is where we know each other from.'* [96]

Rudolf Steiner was known to have echoed this recognition of one master by the other. Ita Wegman, as reported in Zeylmans van Emmichoven's biography, knew Rudolf Steiner's statement that Bulgaria has "its own spiritual teacher."[97] It is clear from this, in conjunction with the statement made to Boyan Boev, that Rudolf Steiner understood that Peter Deunov had a mission to fulfill with the Bulgarian people. In the summer of 1939, Ita Wegman and friends visited Bulgaria and particularly Sofia. They have been hosted by Bulgarian anthroposophist Ekaterina (Katya) Papazova who has connections with followers of Master Peter Deunov. However, there are no evidences for any meetings or comments from Ita Wegman regarding the Master Peter Deunov. Earlier in the summer of 1936, Elizabeth Vreede and Lilli Kolisko visited Sofia on the way to Turkey and returning back through Sofia. They have stopped in Sofia. Also the Orient Express had daily schedule at that time which allowed them to stay, especially on the way back. However, no written documents regarding Master Peter Deunov.

Some take Rudolf Steiner's statement as evidence that Peter Deunov had a local and national mission, and that from this point of view it hardly makes sense to study his activities very seriously, even less so to proffer the thesis that the Maitreya Bodhisattva was manifested through him. Others see in Rudolf Steiner's words an implied meaning and speculate on his proposition that the Master Jesus is working in the 20th century somewhere in the Balkan Carpathian mountain range.[98] This gave rise to specific comments, during Anthroposophical meetings in Bulgaria, that Peter Deunov is probably the Master Jesus. In our opinion there is no sense at all to even dwell on the idea of identifying the Master Peter Deunov with the Master Jesus. Rudolf Steiner had an excellent knowledge of geography and would not have mistaken the names of mountain ranges any more than the names of people. The Master Peter Deunov was widely active on Vitosha Mountain and on Rila Mountain which are within the territory of Bulgaria, not in the Romanian mountain ranges known by the name of the Carpathian Mountains.[99]

It is dangerous to draw unsupported conclusions from Rudolf Steiner's statement about Peter Deunov by comparing his description of the local nature of Peter Deunov's activity with Rudolf Steiner's own conspicuously non-local, Europe-wide activity during the first decades of 20th century. On the contrary, Rudolf Steiner's statement can be interpreted as an indirect indication, a guiding light to the Bodhisattva aspect in the appearance of the Master Beinsa Douno. The point is that a Bodhisattva is the conduit of a strong archangelic impulse and as such he is, before becoming Buddha, strongly connected with and serving the Folk Spirit. From this point of view, if we accept that the Master Beinsa Douno is the manifestation of the Maitreya Bodhisattva in the 20th century, it is only natural that his mission will be strongly connected with one nation or with a group of several nations, and more specifically the Bulgarian nation or the entire family of Slavic nations. In order to see another intimation of a similar national region being the locus of activity of a different Bodhisattva, we can study the example given by Rudolf Steiner when describing the mission of the Bodhisattva Apollo through Orpheus. Rudolf Steiner's words *the Bodhisattva corresponding to Greece*[100] allude to an influence of the Bodhisattva Apollo locally upon the Greek nation and culture. Of course, such a locality, characteristic for a Bodhisattva not yet having completed his mission, does not imply that there are no sublime ideas in the Word of Master Beinsa Douno worthy of serious spiritual-scientific investigation or that in his work and activities there are no esoteric Christian methods of significance to humanity. Unarguably, the Rudolf Steiner's statement mentioned above concerning the mission of Master Beinsa Douno among the Bulgarian people is not only categorical proof that the founder of the Anthroposophical Society is very knowledgeable, duly informed and exceptionally well-read, but it is also a clear sign of the inner bond that exists naturally among those truly initiated in Christ.

Another even more substantial parallel with respect to the issue concerning the national aspect in the manifestation of the Maitreya Bodhisattva in the 20th century is the parallel between the activity of Jeshu ben Pandira and the appearance of the Master Beinsa Douno. It is known that Jeshu ben Pandira worked during the period between the second and first centuries B.C. within a limited territory in Palestine, establishing a small community of followers, the Essene Brotherhood, which according to ancient historians did not number more than 4,000 people.[101] Despite the comparatively small number of followers and the limited geographical and cultural territory of impact, he managed to prepare the physical appearance of Christ-Jesus. We are told both by Rudolf Steiner and by historic sources that the Essenes had a restricted and almost ascetic life-style, which, though organized in communities, was detached from the Greco-Roman culture of that time. (In parallel Rudolf Steiner's followers are around 4,000 in 1920's across Europe). There is a similar aspect with the Teaching of Master Beinsa Douno but among a community of 40,000 people (in 1939), active predominantly within the territory of Bulgaria. Due to the conditions of modern times, that community does not exhibit the asceticism and isolation from contemporary civilization that the Essenes did. It should also be noted that today the Word and path of inner development taught by the Master Beinsa Douno are spreading gradually around the world. Another key element is that the Master Peter Deunov clearly stated that his teaching will focus on the new impulse coming from the Divine World and the Christ Being and manifesting through the powerful Principle of Love. The Master Beinsa Douno says explicitly that the times are so intense that conditions did not allow him to repeat knowledge and concepts already taught by the Masters of humanity but that he would give expression to a teaching that has never before been given. Disciples were assigned the task to investigate on their own and as a group the entire spiritual and esoteric tradition of humankind, taking the following points of departure: (i) the New Divine Teaching based on the Pentagram with the Principles of Love, Wisdom, Truth, Justice and Virtue; (ii) the path of the White Brotherhood (the White Lodge) through the centuries and cultural epochs and (iii) most of all, the activity of the Spirit of Christ driving the entire World Evolution. Such an investigation is crucial because it is only when the disciples know the language, methods and purposes of the esoteric schools that are born in one way or another out of the Christ impulse can the disciples understand what is the new and essential in the Word of the Master who is a herald of the divine world.

As early as the first years of the brotherly life around the spiritual center of *Izgrev* (Bulgarian tr.

Sunrise), the Master Beinsa Douno guided his followers to research valuable and true teachings. He reminded them that contemporary esoteric students coming from the European folks should not apply Indian exercises and practices without transforming and adapting the methods to contemporary human development. This is because, according to the Master Peter Deunov, since the Mystery of the Golgotha we have the opportunity to stop our devolutionary sinking into matter and to start, through the Divine Love of Christ, to drive our development and raise ourselves again up to our true homeland, the spiritual world. Since Indian yogic methods were given during the involutionary period of the development of humanity, they are not appropriate to contemporary Europeans. The Master Beinsa Douno gives a number of exercises and practices analogous to those reaching us from ancient India and representing an evolutionary advance.

It has already been explained that the teaching of the Universal White Brotherhood differs substantially in its ideological aspect from the Theosophical movement guided by the proto-Indian oriented Annie Besant and Charles Leadbeater. Moreover, some disciples had challenging and dangerous experiences when they started making contact with pseudo-Teachings. The Master Beinsa Douno firmly forbade the distribution of the Agni Yoga doctrine and the teaching of Bo Yin Ra in the brotherly community that he founded in Sofia. This categorical tone was occasioned by the fact that no false teachings, directed against the very spirit of Christ, are allowed in the environment of an esoteric school of Christ. Apart from the spiritual movements appearing in ancient times (Brahmanism, Mazdaism, Orphism, Krishnaism, Hermeticism, Essenism, Pythagorism, Bogomilism), which according to the Master Beinsa Douno are all branches of the Universal White Brotherhood whose head is Christ, the disciples naturally were orientated in the esoteric knowledge obtained from contemporary traditions in the stream of the Christ. Some of the most alert and capable disciples of the Master Peter Deunov (Boyan Boev, Vlad Pashov, Georgi Radev, Mihail Ivanov, Metodi Constantinov, etc.) studied anthroposophical sources devotedly and in depth because they found them a closely similar teaching in complete harmony with the principles, laws, and ideas expressed by the Master Beinsa Douno. Moreover, the Master himself stimulated this process in the Bulgarian esoteric school of 20th century by a number of lectures showing all the disciples in his school that Rudolf Steiner is a great initiate of our time. Subsequently, the closest disciples of the Master Peter Deunov have not only been well acquainted with anthroposophical ideas but they have taken an initial step towards a powerful synthesis between the two most closely related esoteric Christian traditions of our time. The present study is a natural result and continuation of this initial synthesis.

The synthesis outlined above between these two European esoteric Christian movements has its methodological significance for inner schooling because, under the strenuous circumstances of the 20th century, disciples must conserve their energy and time. The Master Peter Deunov directed his followers to study the spiritual traditions of humankind, so that they can best prepare for the New Divine Teaching, instilling within oneself life the ability to live in Christ's Love. It happens that this study, as prescribed by the Master, runs most smoothly, effectively, and comprehensively through entering into the ocean of Christ Wisdom called Anthroposophy. This is so because Rudolf Steiner analyzed spiritual-scientifically almost all spiritual traditions in the Light of Christ. The real and essential link between the teaching of the Master Beinsa Douno and Anthroposophy is further shown by the fact that the person who created the conditions for the appearance of Anthroposophy in Bulgaria, by translating many works of Rudolf Steiner, is Dimo Daskalov, one of the followers of the Master Peter Deunov. Dimo Daskalov met the Master Beinsa Douno personally on several occasions; he played songs of the Master on a violin; he conversed closely with Boyan Boev, the close disciple of the Master Beinsa Douno. Dimo Daskalov gave anthroposophical lectures to followers of the Master Peter Deunov. In August 1944, Dimo Daskalov had personal meeting with Master Peter Deunov on Seven

Rila Lakes and received from him the task to translate and make available to Bulgarians Rudolf Steiner's works. Since then he translated tens of volumes and continue doing it for the rest of his life until 1989. This is still to our days the largest Rudolf Steiner's bibliography translated in Bulgarian. The Anthroposophical publishing house in Bulgaria is named after Dimo Daskalov.

There is another methodological similarity between the activities of the spiritual leader Rudolf Steiner and those of the Master Peter Deunov. When presenting the anthroposophical path, Rudolf Steiner explained that the first step of any anthroposophist into the spiritual path is the systematic study of the esoteric truths described by Spiritual Science and experiencing them through oneself. In this way disciples impregnate the sublime wisdom and the living ideas of the Archangel Michael into their soul-spiritual structures. The disciple thereby develops the necessary spiritual organs and senses without which conscious development and progress in Spiritual Science are not possible. A follower of Anthroposophy systematically examines a vast number of profoundly linked ideas, concepts, processes, and functions in the human character and in living nature. He or she also endeavors to experience deeply the essence of the Christ mysteries within the activities of the angelic hierarchies because this is precisely the way to form and manifest the spiritual organs and senses necessary for human evolution.

A key element in approaching Rudolf Steiner's word is not only that there is a certain consistency without which it is impossible to go properly into Anthroposophy: a *method of contemplation* is applied where the widths of the world are left and the striving anthroposophist can deepen his inner life and complete, independently, the picture started by Rudolf Steiner. Thus the spiritual seeker studying anthroposophy naturally develops his inner capacities if he has the courage to ask Parsifal-like questions in the context of the true Rosicrucianism of the 20th century.

Likewise, every unprejudiced and serious researcher of the Word of the Master Peter Deunov observes an internal, immanent code in its structure and essence. For example in the school of esoteric Christianity living among the Bulgarian people, there are the three levels characteristic of occult schools, organized by three kinds of people. The first level consists of followers and listeners who from now on will become aware of the occult principles of esoteric Christianity; the Word intended for them is delivered in the form of Sunday lectures to which access is free. In the second level, the school lectures delivered to the classes of the occult school founded by the Master Beinsa Douno are of a radically different nature and intended for the Faithful (in the esoteric-Christian sense of the word), disciples specially called by the Master Peter Deunov. At the innermost, third level of the School, sacred esoteric processes and relations with the most advanced disciples of the School take place, who are actually direct co-workers and assistants of the Great Master of the Good within the sphere of his work.[102] This is, however, just one type of a structural section of the Esoteric School founded by the Master Beinsa Douno. His very word has specific characteristics and understanding those requires a particular approach.

The first major difference in comparison with the word of Rudolf Steiner that can be seen by the anthroposophical researcher is that the word of the Master Beinsa Douno primarily bears an esoteric-Christian moral character and only secondly an occult-gnostic essence. Therefore, each anthroposophist embarking on an investigation of the word of the Master Beinsa Douno has to tune himself to it differently than to Anthroposophy and above all to approach it impartially and with a pure heart. This is a natural rule generated by the principles of cross-cultural research.[103] The Master Beinsa Douno uses a different approach expressed and woven into his word compared with the method applied by Rudolf Steiner and developed in his books and lectures. If the method applied by Rudolf Steiner can be called a descriptive-co-experiential method and if its objective is to impregnate living Michaelic ideas in the mental microcosm of the spiritual researcher, then the method applied by the Master Beinsa Douno in his word can be regarded as a way to synthesize the widest spectrum of experiences in the uniform texture of the Christ-consciousness. The Master did not select his method accidentally. Its objective is to combine all experiences, from the smallest ones manifested in everyday life to the grandest, eternally transforming experiences that a spiritually seeking person can reach. The Master Beinsa Douno appears in his word as a loving mother teaching her child-disciple by applying the method of conscious mosaic or puzzle arranging. Numerous multi-colored pieces of various shapes fit into one complete overall picture. When this objective is accomplished and, for instance, a lecture (usually devoted to the incredible depth of a line from the Gospel, visually demonstrated by the Master Peter Deunov) is subjected to detailed analysis and esoteric synthesis, the very activity in relating to the arrangement of the lecture, by acquiring a deeper understanding of its content, through reflection, and through meditative contemplation entering more deeply into the Word, has an unusually purifying and transforming effect on the soul-spiritual structures of the researcher. This is, in its essence, a direct appearance of the Christ Spirit within the space of the 'I'-hood of the disciple. Actually every lecture or speech of the Master Beinsa Douno is not only a conceptual-reasoning challenge but primarily a moral ray of the Christ Light directed to the esoteric disciple's consciousness soul, a microcosm of the Second Appearance of the Christ within the human soul, a universe into which one can enter only if one approaches it with a sacred attitude and serious esoteric preparation in the Michael science of today.

It is precisely here where the deep bond between the two true schools of esoteric Christianity appearing in the 20th century can be observed: if a person has undergone serious anthroposophical preparation, he will get more deeply, and much more completely, into the Christian transforming essence of the word of the Master Beinsa Douno. On the other hand, if a spiritual disciple has long practiced and developed Christian virtues with the help of the word of the Master Beinsa Douno, such a disciple much more naturally and intensively perceives, experiences, and applies the ideas that the great initiate Rudolf Steiner developed in Anthroposophy. In the Western esoteric school, one can find the fundamental Michaelic elements of esotericism; in the Eastern school of esoteric Christianity, one can contemplate the complex compounds and living tissues formed by these elements, combined in the context of the Gospel. In this way, the Ahrimanic opposition to the development of Michaelic virtues in European cultural conditions is overcome and conquered, and, as Master Beinsa Douno pointed out, a divine science is created having two major parts, one esoteric-cognitive and the other moral-practical. It is particularly this powerful methodological synthesis between the above-mentioned parts of the approaches to spiritual-scientific research of the two branches of esoteric Christianity that can preserve and focus in an appropriate direction the light of the Michael wisdom newly acquired by humanity.

The two schools of contemporary esoteric Christianity and, more precisely, the two ways of speaking of their leaders are not contradictory but, to the contrary, are in a deep and sacred unity, serving one single and sacred objective: the Reappearance of Christ in the human soul, in the soul of humanity.

These natural relationships between the two esoteric Christian traditions of the 20th century have deep historic roots. According to the Master Beinsa Douno, the great initiates of humanity, the great Masters and Heralds of the Universal White Brotherhood, in the process of their work throughout the centuries, have formed three branches of the Esoteric School of the White Brotherhood.[104] The first branch is called the *Egyptian Branch*. It appeared in Egypt, then in Persia and Greece, and had the aim of preparing the spiritual conditions in the Caucasian race for the Christianity of the future. The second branch can be called the *Palestinian*. It originated from the Egyptian branch, spread with the Essenes in Palestine and moved to Rome, England and Germany during the Christian epoch. It had the aim of introducing and spreading Christianity throughout the world. The third branch can be called the *Bogomilian*. Starting from Egypt, it went into India and then to Persia, Syria, Arabia, Asia Minor and Slavic

Bulgaria. This branch has the aim of applying the Divine Teaching, i.e. esoteric Christianity. In the early Middle Ages, the third branch spread actively in Europe. Although the Bogomils were subjected to persecution, murdered and burnt at the stake, they spread a powerful spiritual wave all over Europe through their later European appearances in the Albigensians and Cathars. The Master Beinsa Douno emphasizes that Rosicrucianism, as an esoteric denomination, is a branch of the *Bogomilian* branch coming to Europe through Bulgaria. This is also supported by the anthroposophical research of Christopher Bamford in his introduction to Rudolf Steiner's lectures on Rosicrucianism,[105] in which it is mentioned that Christian Rosenkreutz was most likely born on the border between Hesse and Thuringia into a Cathar family and brotherly community, which points to the profound spiritual and historical links between the esoteric denominations of the Bogomils, the Cathars, and the Rosicrucians.

The teaching of the Master Beinsa Douno renews and further develops the Bulgarian esoteric tradition with the aim of preparing it as a seed and a foundation for the Slavic cultural epoch, while Anthroposophy is the renewed core of Rosicrucianism, the esoteric center for central and western Europe. It is only natural that there are deep internal links between these two spiritual traditions arising from common roots and ideals and lasting into the present.

Forging the sacred link between the two impulses of the contemporary esoteric Christianity, the western and the eastern impulses, the fiery synthesis between the true Rosicrucianism of today and the Word of the Bodhisattva Maitreya is one of the sacred principles motivating any sincere seeker onto the Path pointed to by the radiant eyes of the Archangel Michael.

7. Are there any other significant signs, ideas, or conclusions on the matter of the Maitreya Bodhisattva that can further orient the spiritual-scientific researcher?

We shall indicate briefly some supplementary conclusions and ideas that throw light on the matter:

7.1. Rudolf Steiner stated unambiguously that the Maitreya Bodhisattva brings, prepares, and manifests the innermost understanding of all necessary concepts and details regarding the Mystery of Golgotha. Apart from this, in the same lecture in which Rudolf Steiner discloses some of the most important details about the mission of the Maitreya Bodhisattva (Leipzig, 4 November 1911, GA 130), he also hints at an important key, a kind of verbal password: *the Impulse of Christ is power and life...* This points to the intimate center of the esoteric Christianity contemplated by the twelve Bodhisattvas. It is a key to the discovery of the word of the 20th century Bodhisattva, namely that that word provides us with orientation to the present activity of the Christ Being. Any follower of the teaching of the Master

Peter Deunov is intimately familiar with this. To every Bulgarian cultural researcher, the phrase *power and life* is synonymous with the basis of the Master's teaching and with the esoteric understanding of the Gospel texts. This has its historic grounds: when people asked the Master Peter Deunov at what point to start studying his teaching, he guided his followers to the published talks in six volumes, titled *Power and Life (1914-1924)*.[106] In this book, almost all the lines from the Gospels are examined in the greatest detail from the esoteric-Christian point of view. Rudolf Steiner's lectures provide the best orientation available about the mission of the Bodhisattva in the present time; within the intimate teaching about the Christ contained in these lectures, he has given one of the main methods by which we can recognize the Bodhisattva: the Bodhisattva contemplates and obtains inspiration for his word from the power and life of the Christ. This is why the Word of the Bodhisattva will lead souls to the power and life of the Christ, the Word of the Bodhisattva will be called *power and life*. Indeed, there is one Master in the 20th century who explicitly called his word *power and life*.

7.2. Spiritual Science has provided sufficient information about the fact that, at the end of 19th century, a new Golgotha mystery in is process but now in the spiritual world. The very intense materialistic deviations of humanity from its spiritual reality brought about a new crucifixion of the Christ Being. Since 1930, humanity has been developing and become more able to see and experience this Christ in an etheric body because a new Christ sacrifice and new Resurrection took place. Rudolf Steiner predicted that, at around the middle of the fourth decade of the 20th century, humanity will face the Beast coming from the infernal abyss.[107]

There is absolutely clear information directly linked with the life of the Master Peter Deunov about a sublime mystery that took place in 1936 and was directly linked with the new sacrifice of the Christ Being and His Reappearance in the etheric. It appears that a sort of projection of the New Golgotha is occurring, directed at the 20th century Bodhisattva because he is in a constant contemplative relation with the Spirit of Christ. In this case also, the events that have transpired in the etheric realm since the death of Rudolf Steiner confirm the extraordinary depth of his clairvoyance.

7.3. It is known from the indications provided by Rudolf Steiner that the Master appearing through Jeshu ben Pandira was one of the leaders of the Essene brotherhood, the healing brotherhood. The Essenes aspired to purification of the soul, of the body, and of the blood through a number of spiritual practices, in accordance with which they refrained from eating meat and drinking alcohol. In this way, they not only maintained their personal spiritual hygiene but mastered the healing art of individual inner perfection. Rudolf Steiner emphasized that the new appearance of this

Master would bring a renewed Essenism directed to the particular manifestation of the Etheric Christ.[108] It is only natural to suppose that certain typical features of Essenian teaching will be radiating again in the activities of the 20th century Bodhisattva. And indeed his life shows this: the Master Peter Deunov was known as a healer; he miraculously healed thousands of people. Several cases were described which were interpreted as resurrection by his followers but this was not made widely known because he emphasized that this could have led to an interruption of his mission. This correlates to Rudolf Steiner's assertion that the Bodhisattva will not proclaim himself.[109]

Another not less significant sign is one of the spiritual traditions applied naturally by the Brotherhood of Light in Bulgaria. Under the guidance of the Master Peter Deunov, ideological vegetarianism is practiced; out of love and compassion for our smaller brothers, the animals; food obtained as a result of killing is not eaten. Apart from this approach to eating and along with abstinence from drinking alcohol, many other methods for the purification of the blood and the body are applied. These are not special ritualistic forms aiming at the salvation of small groups of people, but rather a broad spectrum of methods for conscious purification and salvation of all people and, together with them, the entire animal kingdom.

7.4. Rudolf Steiner makes clear that contemporary humanity undergoes a sort of initiation with a partly or fully conscious mastering of the functions of the astral body, i.e. humanity makes efforts to develop the Spirit-Self. However, only the disciple of an esoteric Christian school makes conscious efforts to transform the habits and customs, the so-called character or second nature of the human being, in a way that is aimed at developing higher faculties. The conscious balancing of character and habits is actually a conscious harmonization and mastering of the etheric body, which leads to the development of the second principle of the spirit within us, the life-spirit. Exactly as predicted by Rudolf Steiner, the 20th century Bodhisattva, the Master Peter Deunov, laid great emphasis on this aspect in the esoteric school that he founded. Some of the primary objectives set before the disciples of the White Brotherhood are aimed at mastering consciousness regarding all those functions of the *second nature* (the innate approach to thinking, feeling, and willing as well as conscious processes related to eating, breathing, sleeping and so on) completely permeating them with the Spirit of Christ. Important tasks were assigned to develop *good habits,* a noble and balanced character fulfilled with Christ virtues.

The entire teaching of the Bodhisattva of the Good, the entire approach of the Master Beinsa Douno, cultivates the fruitful transformation, taking place in the *disciple's soul*, of the wisdom of the Eightfold Path (*right thinking, right reflection, right word, right deed,* and so on) into an overwhelming and abundant power of love given through the drops of the Blood of Christ in the Holy Chalice. A hundred years before the Common Era, the Bodhisattva preached and worked for the physical appearance of the Christ; now he preaches and works with a particular methodology to foster the appearance of the etheric Christ in the human soul and in the traits and daily life of the Disciple of the Esoteric Christian School. When the disciples consciously master their etheric body, they are actually preparing for the point of contact and contemplation of the Second Appearance of Christ in an etheric form. The Bodhisattva, through Jeshu ben Pandira, worked in the past for the physically manifested body and blood of Christ; now the Master Beinsa Douno teaches us through intimate Grail mysteries how Christ's *power and life* can become our own flesh and blood. Because after approximately three thousand years, the Maitreya Buddha will seek people who live according to the following conviction: *Not only is my head filled with the wisdom of the Eightfold Path, I have not only the teaching, the wisdom of love, but my heart is full of the living substance of love, of that which overflows and streams out into the world.* And Rudolf Steiner continues, saying of these people: *With such human beings will the Maitreya Buddha then be able to carry out his further mission in the progressive evolution of the world.*[110] The Gautama Buddha brought the teaching of love and compassion; the Master Beinsa Douno comes to give us the teaching about the practical life in the love of Christ:

In my mind, I carry the idea of the good of the whole of humanity. I think not only about the good of the all humankind but also about the good of animals and plants. I wish for all beings to live in love and to acquire virtues. I know that God lives in every soul and I want not a single wrong thought to remain in their consciousness. I came to teach people how to live in Love.[111]

7.5. The sacred aim for which Master Beinsa Douno works can be achieved by applying various esoteric Christian methods. One of the most important among them is the musical approach of the Master Peter Deunov. There is no other spiritual Master in the 20th century that has such rich musical activity in his manifestation. He gave humanity about one hundred musical pieces, which he called *occult musical exercises*. This is not a coincidence but rather an important aspect of the contemporary work of the White Lodge. The 'I' of humanity, the Christ through His holy organs of wisdom, the twelve Bodhisattvas, works most intensively for the formation of the *consciousness soul* within the human being. We know from Rudolf Steiner[112] that the soul develops predominantly from the occult power of music. The Bodhisattva Apollo, as he manifested through

Orpheus in the region of Thrace on the Balkan Peninsula, worked through this approach. He illumined people through his music in order to develop the intellectual-logical aspect of their souls. Almost 3500 years after the manifestation of the individual mission of the Bodhisattva Apollo, a new impulse appeared on the Balkan Peninsula, radiated by the Lodge of the Bodhisattvas and again through music. Now the Maitreya Bodhisattva works through his original musical pieces for violin and voice, already manifested in one esoteric Christian school. The activity of the Bodhisattva Apollo was directed methodologically mainly toward the intellectual soul in order to prepare the day-waking capacity of thinking in humanity, so that it could receive properly the impulse of the approaching physical manifestation of the Christ Spirit; the work of the Maitreya Bodhisattva, manifested through Peter Deunov during the first half of 20th century, is again focused in his method through music, but now towards the consciousness soul. The new aim is to become conscious of the Etheric Appearance of Christ in the microcosm of the human being.

7.6. We know from spiritual science that the Maitreya Bodhisattva will fulfill his mission and become the Maitreya Buddha in the middle of the sixth, the Slavic, cultural epoch.[113] This is an indirect indication leads us to look for the impulse of the 20th century

Bodhisattva in a Slavic country of rich esoteric culture. Moreover, according the words of the Bodhisattva, his *mission is related to the new path of the Slavs and to the coming of the Sixth Race.*[114] All of this provides grounds to believe that the specific characteristics of the Slavs and of the sixth epoch can be reliable points for a more profound understanding of the activity of the 20th century Bodhisattva.

According to Rudolf Steiner, the East Europeans and particularly the Slavs continue to have the capacity to perceive the etheric energy of living, intelligent nature. This makes them rather different from more western people. The Slavs are, so to say, *behind the times, underdeveloped*[115] in descending into matter and can still contemplate the living God in nature. It is opinion of the authors that the 20th century Bodhisattva makes use of this particular underdevelopment as a point of support for the acceleration of the development of the Slavic organism of the Bulgarian people for the sake of the Etheric Appearance of Christ. The so-called *musical* method,[116] completely different in this usage from the conventional meaning of "music", finds its practical and applicable forms in the activity of the Master Peter Deunov within the regular Brotherhood Assembly (and still continuing) and excursions into the scenic nature of Bulgaria motivated by spiritual ideals. The Brotherhood was taught, solely through the extraordinarily powerful presence of the Master Beinsa Douno, to contemplate the activities of *living intelligent nature* and to work in cooperation with and to assist Nature. In this way, the etheric bodies of the Slavs are being prepared by a means related to nature for the event of the Etheric Appearance of Christ.

Western esoteric disciples working with spiritual knowledge live predominantly in urbanized environments, as does most of the population, where it can be difficult to look for the wisdom of the initiates impregnated in living nature. Very much in contrast, the Eastern Esoteric Disciple experiences the Christ School annually in the natural-mystic environment of the *Seven Rila Lakes,* which give an impressive picture of and symbolize the seven-tiered structures of existence and the human being. This approach of the Master Peter Deunov contributes to the development of the etheric body and brings about at the same time, through the powers of the etheric body that are being fostered, of a new type of consciousness, the collective consciousness of the brothers and sisters in Christ. Through the methodology of living in brotherly communities, souls can try to practice the life of the early Christians, inspired by the *power and life* of the Christ. Thus they are preparing to become the embryo of the sixth great epoch and as living, conscious cells form the body and the soul organism of the Etheric Christ.

7.7. If the mission of Gautama Buddha did not include the development of the entire Consciousness Soul, but only a part of it, namely the ethics of love and compassion,[117] then the teaching of the Master Beinsa Douno is mainly about the path of development of a new type of a human being, a human being living in full consciousness that one is studying in the *Great School of Life*. This is the human being – *Disciple* in the meaning of Beinsa Douno. This term denotes nothing else but an esoteric analogy or synonym of the concept of *Consciousness Soul*.

Being aware of this parallel we can realize another fact regarding the activity of the 20th century Bodhisattva: any unbiased researcher of the Teaching of the Master Peter Deunov can say that there is no other known Master who had spoken in so much detail and so consistently, so broadly and comprehensively on the principle of Divine Love. At the same time, the Master Beinsa Douno points out that the thousands of lectures and talks delivered on this topic are merely an introduction to the Great Divine Science of Love. On the one hand, this is because Christ is the Principle of Love, and understanding love, we shall understand the present and eternal activity of the Spirit of Christ. However, on the other hand, particularly today in the epoch of the consciousness soul, a macrocosmic impulse is manifested coming from the Brothers of Love, the Seraphim. Apart from being the most supreme principle in the angelic hierarchies, they simultaneously become a macrocosmic principle of the consciousness soul in the soul-cosmic organism[118] of the *Heavenly Christ, the Great Cosmic Human Being.*

Precisely with the purpose of being in resonance with the Beings of Universal Love, who organize the social life of the solar systems in our Galaxy, the Herald of the Holy Spirit assists in the dawning and spreading of a new epoch, the epoch of the conscious disciple of Divine Love, the Epoch of the Consciousness Soul. This is, in its essence, the very microcosmic core of the Second Appearance of the Christ Being. And here we would like to offer a new point of view.* It is known that the Bodhisattvas are deeply related internally with the hierarchies of Archangels and Dynamis (Powers).[119] On the other hand it is known that the Maitreya Bodhisattva's mission begins from the epoch of the intellectual soul, finishes in the epoch of the prophetic development of the Spirit-Self, while in the present, it runs in the epoch of the consciousness soul. For that reason, a connection can be made that the 20th century Bodhisattva's mission will embrace and bear the Loving Seraphic Flame of the Cosmic 'I'—the Christ.[120]

Intelligent nature has implanted a number of keys of wisdom in the structure of the human being. For example, for an observer to distinguish a three-dimensional reality, binocular sight is needed, i.e., simultaneous and synchronized observation from two different points of view. Applying this particular approach in our spiritual-scientific research about the mission of the 20th century Bodhisattva, we can understand the volume and in-depth key details in the present spiritual conditions. Synchronizing the Michael points of view of the two impulses of contemporary esoteric Christianity we can actually touch upon the Reappearance of the Christ in the Etheric.

One of the most important additional ideas arising from working in this way is that the activity of the Maitreya Bodhisattva will not only be preaching about the Reappearance of the Christ but will also provide the practical means for making it possible for the Etheric Christ to appear in the 'I'-space of the disciple, particularly under the conditions of a brotherly community life. In other words: succeeding with the practical work given by the 20th-century Bodhisattva will, in fact, be the Reappearance of the Christ in the Etheric: it will be the esoteric Christian initiation of the new epoch.

Therefore, like sailors who determine their position on the sea by three bright stars, we shall present clear evidence of the significant place of the teaching and methodology of the Master Beinsa Douno in world spiritual culture through three methods radiating Christ's light and given by 20th century Bodhisattva: *The*

Pentagram, The Testament of the Color Rays of Light, and Paneurhythmy.

7.8. The Pentagram is the symbol of the teaching of the Master Peter Deunov. It is formed by five rays upon the five Divine Principles of Love, Wisdom, Truth, Justice, and Virtue, and a circle encompassing the rays. Upon this circle is written the mystic formula: *In fulfilling God's Will is the power of the human soul.* The imagination represented in the pentagram with a tip pointing upwards was first given in a black and white drawing in 1910. (Note that this is also the beginning of the period, according to Sergei Prokofieff, of the strongest spiritual influence of the Maitreya Bodhisattva upon Rudolf Steiner by way of inspiration.) Later this was also given as an exceptionally vivid painting in 1922, the year the Esoteric School of Christ opened on Earth. The painting of the Pentagram also contains additional rich symbols, which in general represent the Path of the Disciple in the Esoteric School of Christ. This imagination, symbolizing the core of the teaching of the Master Beinsa Douno, is actually one of the most powerful signs that he is indeed the 20th century Bodhisattva. We shall briefly give only a few of our considerations related to this matter:

(i) The Christianized tradition of the Jewish Kabbalah, related directly with the Essene Brotherhood, spells and records the name of

Jeshu (הושהי), as a derivative of the four-letter Name of God (הוהי), in the form of the Pentagram. The one who appeared through Jeshu ben Pandira and who served Jeshu (Jesus) of Nazareth appeared in the 20th century as well and selected the Pentagram as a sign of his renewed teaching.

(ii)   The Pentagram is a sign of the manifestation of the hierarchy of the Archangels because the sign of the Pentagram is written in the cosmic sphere of Venus (up to which the Archangels appear), inscribed by the very movement of Venus correlated with the movement of the Earth, the Sun and the fixed stars. As mentioned above, any Bodhisattva is intimately related with the activities of the Archangels; it is natural therefore for the 20th century Bodhisattva to symbolize this cosmic and hierarchical correlation in the Pentagram, the symbol-imagination given by him.

(iii)   The Bodhisattva who appears in 20th century, serving the Etheric Appearance of the Christ, places the Pentagram as the sign describing the mystic path before the disciple's soul because the Pentagram with its five rays symbolizes this fifth, 20th-century sacrifice of the Christ through Nathan's soul in the name of humanity.

(iv) The necessity is known from Anthroposophy to form a sort of protective skeleton in the etheric body of the disciple, so that the disciple can be protected by the spiritual world from the disharmonic influences of the opposing spiritual beings. The skeleton of the etheric body acquires the form of a pentagram.[121] The 20th century Bodhisattva irradiates the esoteric school founded by him with a powerful imagination in the form of a Pentagram not only because he wants to defend and protect his followers but also because he wants to stimulate the development of the etheric body aimed at preparing the disciple for the forthcoming Etheric Appearance of the Christ.

(v) It is again Anthroposophy that teaches us that the pentagram is a symbol of the activity of the third principle of the Trinity, the Holy Spirit.[122] The 20th century Bodhisattva is a Herald of the Holy Spirit on the Earth and this is why he expresses his contemporary appearance through the Pentagram.

We can draw the conclusion that the herald of the Lodge of the Bodhisattva in 20th century, the Master Beinsa Douno, renewed the form of the pentagram and transformed it into a central method of his contemporary esoteric Christian school.

7.9. *The Testament of the Color Rays of Light* is the method that the Master Beinsa Douno received personally from Christ when he underwent a crucial experience.[123] Master Beinsa Douno reached a new level of initiation in Christ and in 1912 gave humanity a universal method for enhancing the soul and the etheric body with virtues. This method works through reflection and meditation upon specially selected texts from the *Book of our Lord,* the Bible, by the principle of light-and-color selection. The Word of God written down through the centuries in the Judeo-Christian sacred book has its own spectral code. The Bodhisattva who inspired the knowledge within the community of the Essenes that is given in the Gospel of Matthew regarding the preparation of the physical and etheric bodies of Jesus through forty-two generations[124] – that Bodhisattva is working now for the realization of the shining Etheric Appearance in spiritual glowing Light. He reveals to us how through the hues of the rainbow (the external etheric forms) and through the virtues of the soul (the internal etheric content and current of forces) are manifested the Supreme Creators of Light – the Spirits of Fire and Light.[125] The Master Beinsa Douno teaches us that the different types of external light are only the garments of spiritual principles, beings such as *the Spirit of Love, the Spirit of*

Life, the Spirit of Holiness, the Spirit of Wisdom, the Spirit of Eternity, the Spirit of Truth, the Spirit of Power, etc. Virtues stream from them indispensable for the disciple following the steps of the Resurrected Lord. The Master Beinsa Douno, emanating this new Christ method, said in 1912 (during the period when the spiritual inspiration of the Maitreya Bodhisattva upon Rudolf Steiner was at its strongest, according to Sergei Prokofieff [126]) the following:

> *I want to form a strong wave of the seven colors because Christ is near the physical field. And he is present this year at the Assembly. All these verses [comprising the Testament of the Color Rays of Light] are taken out under His guidance, therefore always, when you use them, God will help you.... Christ has never been present in the way He was present this year....* [127]

Indications given by Rudolf Steiner allow us to recognize this particular approach taken by the Master Beinsa Douno as a manifestation of the Maitreya Bodhisattva. The founder of the Anthroposophical Movement describes in great detail how the Archangels, the Sons of Fire, acquired their human stage of development on the Ancient Sun through the emanation and manifestation of light. [128] It is known that the development of the Bodhisattvas is profoundly and intimately related with the Archangelic Hierarchy and the stage of development of the Solar System called the *Ancient Sun*. All these facts, taken together, allow us to understand more clearly and in greater detail the mysterious prediction of Rudolf Steiner: *Oriental mysticism was able to picture the consequences of that event but not the actual form which it would take. The mind could picture that within 5,000 years after the great Buddha achieved enlightenment, pure Akashic forms, bathed in fire, lit by sun, would appear in the wake of One beyond the ken of oriental mysticism...something would happen to make it possible for the Sons of Fire and Light to move about the earth, not in physical embodiment but as pure Akashic forms within the earth's moral atmosphere. But then, so it was said, in 5,000 years after Gautama Buddha's enlightenment, the teacher will also be there to make known to men the nature of these wonderful forms of pure fire and light. This teacher – the Maitreya Buddha – will appear 3,000 years after our present era and will be able to teach the Christ impulse....Even now there proceed from him who later on will be the Maitreya Buddha the most significant teachings concerning the Christ Being and the sons of the fire – the Agnishvattas – of Indian mysticism.*[129]

As the founder of spiritual science predicted, there is one Bodhisattva who appeared with great moral power in the 20th century and who gives a supreme spiritual method to humanity for connecting with the Etheric Christ and the Spirits of Fire and Light (the

112

Archangels)—a method which is shaped by the sacred *Word of God* written eternally in the *Book of Life* as *pure Akashic forms.* It seems that each line, each word, ever pronounced on the Earth by the Holy Spirit finds its place in the *Testament of the Color Rays of Light* and becomes a sacred aura, a sacred suite of that Master who is a Herald of the Lodge of the Bodhisattvas. In other words, *the Testament of the Color Rays of Light* is one sacred ray from the commencing dawn of that great event which will be spreading ever stronger and stronger and will culminate in its peak might after about three thousand years. Namely this pivotal event will be the preaching of the First Christ Enlightened, teaching humankind in the never-ending Wisdom about how Light becomes Virtue, and Virtue – accomplished Christ Love.

7.10. Speaking the word *Paneurhythmy* we cannot miss the similarity in sound to the name of the spiritual practice of *eurythmy* given to humanity by Rudolf Steiner. Obviously, it is an esoteric key* set by the two great initiates. It can be found only if a Michaelic synthesis is made between the two branches of the contemporary Esoteric Christianity: the Eastern one—the teaching of the Great Universal Brotherhood, and the Western one—Anthroposophy.

---

* "Key" in the sense of a key to esoteric understanding, as a cryptographic key enables us to understand what has been encrypted.

In order to understand Paneurhythmy, given to us by the Master Beinsa Douno, we have to be familiar with eurythmy and to understand it, in other words, to know what the practice of eurythmy entails. On the other hand if we want to understand how eurythmic principles develop in a complete etheric architecture, we have to examine Paneurhythmy as a unique phenomenon in the contemporary European Christian culture.

The authors of this study wish that every reader motivated in good faith would have the chance to climb the ancient mountain of Rila on the Balkan peninsula on an August 19th and on eagle's wings fly over the seven mountain chakras, called the *Seven Rila Lakes,* and specifically over the spacious field at the fifth lake, known by the mystic Vatan[130] name of *Mahabur.* On this date each year, every sincere follower of contemporary Esoteric Christianity can contemplate and at the same time participate in the grand spiritual phenomenon taking place at an altitude of over 2000 meters (6500 feet): a thousand people coming from all over the planet, against the background of mystic music and songs, form beautiful geometrical figures and in this way they build, through their dances, the body of a living etheric temple, created by the 20th century Bodhisattva. Under the flames of the Michaelic synthesis and consciously led by the Spirit of Paneurhythmy, let us for a moment enter together the space under the arches of this sanctuary built by thousands of brothers and sisters in Christ and contemplate together the meaning and content of its wonderful forms.[131]

Paneurhythmy, this contemporary esoteric Christian practice (methodology), unfolded gradually in three stages and was born during the period 1930-1942. The 20th century Bodhisattva gave it to humanity through an Eastern European Slavic people in an epochal moment in planetary evolution, at the beginning of the period of the supersensible manifestation of the Redeemer. As Rudolf Steiner himself pointed out, the true brotherhoods developed under the conditions of the East, and it is known from Anthroposophy that the Spirit-Self will dawn in the Slavic people of Eastern Europe in the sixth cultural epoch. In other words, Paneurhythmy can be contemplated as a concrete manifestation of the nascent new Aquarian culture – a culture of highly developed collective consciousness. It is only ever practiced in groups, unlike eurythmy, which is an individual practice (though it can, of course, be performed in a group as well). This is why Paneurhythmy as a collective method is particularly directed to the etheric body, and in a way different from eurythmy. Undoubtedly, both practices have as a purpose to prepare and ennoble the etheric body so that it can be suitable for the new manifestation of the Christ Spirit in etheric forms in the highest regions of the astral world.

On the one hand, Paneurhythmy has a direct relevance for the new level of consciousness that gradually and ever more strongly awakens in humanity – the day-waking collective consciousness that will develop in the future Slavic epoch. This is evidenced by the fact that the correct performance of Paneurhythmy requires not only a good deal of self-control but also complete unity and harmony within the entire group of conscious souls engaging in this dynamic practice of contemporary esoteric Christianity. On the other hand, Paneurhythmy can be well viewed as one of the first rays of the dawn called *the Etheric Reappearance of the Christ,* not only because it started appearing precisely during the exceptionally significant period for humankind, described by Rudolf Steiner, but also because in this practice one can see the characteristics typical of a new type of collective consciousness permeated by the Christ Spirit. To show this, we shall quote a small part of the beautiful lyrics in Exercise 23 of the first part of Paneurhythmy:

> *Every beautiful divine day*
> *I breathe joy and life.*
> *A smile comes onto my face*
> *That I am loved by the Lord.*
> *With Love does the Sun*
> *Caress my face*
> *And the loving voice of Christ*
> *Whispers in my heart:*
> *"Firm and brave you live your Life*

To be able to help the world.
You should praise with songs of joy
The Love of God –
Loving and Holy Father of ours,
Known to all souls."

The very name of this fundamental method of eastern esoteric Christianity supposes that what we witness here is a completely developed, in a remarkable scope, method for eurythmization. Indeed, *Pan-eurhythmy* is a *total vital rhythm,* aimed at setting in motion and evolution all seven spiritual levels in the totality of the human being. As if the graceful geometrical figures, outlined by the motions of the performers, elevate and bless the physical body in a very special way. The power flows, set in motion by the rhythmic group work of thousands of people, synchronized with the work of the larynx and with the motions of the limbs, runs through the etheric body and structures it. The performers work consciously with their imagination by perceiving, building freely, and maintaining beautiful images in their consciousness; and thus they elevate their astral body. The mystic tender melody harmonizes the mental activity of the human individuality, while the poetic words bring in the Daylight of the Manas-hood-like dawning of our Spirit-Self. Dancing Paneurhythmy, one starts cultivating and endowing mankind's fruit of one's virtues from the etheric garden called Life-Spirit. In the end, *the total-*

117

living-rhythm may assist us here on the physical level, to experience intuitively the cosmic reality of the Christ Being and thus to work in a prophetic way for our transformation into Spirit-humans.

Paneurhythmy is something unusually ancient and simultaneously only the beginning of a radically new type of phenomenon in human culture that will develop from now on into the distant future. Expert choreographers know that certain areas in the world have, from ancient times, retained a particular practice for preserving human experience and knowledge: in the entirety of sequential, precisely determined movements, the history of a people, for instance, or a legend about the life of a supreme being is recorded. Examples of this ancient practice of similar choreographic writing can still be found among the people of the islands of Hawaii and Tahiti and in the tradition of the Indian dance.[132]

Rudolf Steiner gave something similar through spiritual science in an art of movement that expresses spoken sounds, musical tones, astrological signs, etc. The eurythmic forms are composed of the combinations of movements expressing in an exact way each sound, sign, planet, and so on, so that a picture of an entire poetic, musical, or dramatic work can be given in movement. On the other hand, Master Peter Deunov, giving Paneurhythmy to humanity, combines precisely determined motions that follow a strict sequential line, musical background and poetic context. This totality of music, songs, poetry, movements, and prayers is always performed in the same way not because it is a narrow phenomenon but because it represents a complete esoteric text, a whole etheric architecture having a strictly defined geometry, structure, and meaning. What would it happen if some of the pillars in the Cathedral in Chartres changed place or if they were made of another material less strong and stable? Centuries have elapsed since the construction of this temple, but it has always been one and the same for dozens of generations of people who have seen and entered it. By analogy it can be said that Paneurhythmy is an etheric temple, built by living, collectively conscious people. This temple is in fact a whole organism of a precisely determined structure, sustainable through time, and has a physiology formed by movements permeated by the eurythmic principle. Paneurhythmy is literally an esoteric book given by the Maitreya Bodhisattva of the 20th century. It is written not with paper and ink but it is being written continually in the organism of the planet through the etheric currents of the collective brotherly life in Christ. For some decades this living temple, this living book, has spread into many countries in the world and been practiced by thousands of people, yet it is only today that we begin to examine its meaning, its contents, and its form from a spiritual-scientific point of view.

Many things can be said about Paneurhythmy but the most significant – experiencing Paneurhythmy as a reality – can be achieved only in direct contact with it. Paneurhythmy, this monumental initiating temple of the Etheric Reappearance of the Christ, built by the Maitreya Bodhisattva in a miraculous way, awaits, with doors open wide, the souls of courageous, inquiring, and devoted seekers among those belonging to the School of Michael.

What this book cannot give is the direct experience of the work of the Master Beinsa Douno. Our hope is that our readers will look for that experience, both in the written work of the Master and the community experience of members of the White Brotherhood.

Until recently, access to the word of the Master Beinsa Douno was very difficult due to limited number of translations. However, this number is growing. Lectures can be accessed at:

http://PeratDanov.com

http://Beinsa.bg

http://BeinsaDouno.org

We shall conclude this chapter with two original quotations of the word of Master Beinsa Douno regarding the Second Appearance of the Christ, as we send with a brotherly greeting in Christ to every anthroposophist seeking the word and the mysteries of the Maitreya Bodhisattva![133]

The Living Christ is the manifestation of God, the manifestation of Love. Neither in the outer Cosmos, not in the inner mystic depth of the soul, is there a more comprehensive manifestation of Love than the one we personify in Christ. Christ, with His coming to the earth, wanted to make Divine Love visible. He could not express it in words. Not only before Christ, but also after Christ, there was no human being having Love greater than His. This is what Christ wanted—to express Divine Love and to bring it to the Earth. Christ brought Love into the world. Christ came to the earth to bring Love. He is Love.

By saying Christ, I understand a Being that has overwhelming Love for humanity and wants to give humanity the value that being has in its self, this is the aim of Christ.

As the energy of the sun does not reach us directly but passes through etheric space, in the same way does Divine Love reach people through Christ, who appears as a herald of Love. Christ can be likened in part to the beautiful and luminous image of the sun.

He is the Great Inspirer of all revelations through all time! He is the invisible motive power of the entire spiritual life of humanity. He endured profanations, blows, the Cross, the nails, the spears. With the flame of

Love, He melted the weapons of violence—and His attempt was a success. During His coming two thousand years ago, Christ showed us only one side of His image. We see Christ in humiliations and grief, in sufferings and trials—we see Him as a hero of redemption. People do not know yet Christ in His glory, in His divine power and might. Mighty and powerful is Christ now.

In the past, Christ's hand was pierced with a nail, but today no one can pierce this hand with nails: they will instantly melt.

In the past, Christ was crucified, but today there is no tree big enough on which He can be crucified. Christ cannot be crucified again.

This Christ is coming now to visit human minds and hearts. He will destroy all prisons; will obliterate all the false teachings—all that destroys the human mind and heart, which fills human beings with confusion and lack of principles, which cripples human life. Christ will visit every person. He is the Living Christ, Who brings Life, Light and Freedom for all souls, Who inspires and awakes Love to everything. When we say that Christ is coming now, some think that He will come from the outside. Christ will not come from the outside. He will not appear either in human or in any other form whatsoever. When the rays of the sun enter your home, does this mean that the sun has visited you? Remember that Christ is a manifestation of the love of God. And He will come as an internal light in the minds and hearts of people. This light will draw everyone around Christ as a great center. The opening of human minds and hearts and the reception of Christ within—this will be the Second Appearance of Christ on the earth. He will preach mainly the great science of love and the way to apply it. He will preach the path of discipleship, brotherhood, and serving. Because this is what the law of evolution requires today.

Prepare to meet Christ! Prepare so that everybody in his own time can meet Christ. Put on your new clothes. For some, Christ will come even today, for others— tomorrow, for others still—in years. You will see Him when you are prepared. Receive Christ in your hearts as a friend, and in your mind—as Teacher. Christ is working now.

Christ's impulse will penetrate gradually into the human being and will take over the guidance of the further development of the humanity. We are still at the beginning of this now.

In the future, Christianity—not the external, official Christianity, but the mystic, esoteric Christianity—will become a world religion for the whole of humanity. Christ will be placed in the center of the new culture.

Love as a great principle should be manifested in the human soul, and only then we can unify with Christ. One thing is required from all people—to get connected with Christ. Once you unite with Him, He will be with you until the end of time. He is a gate leading the human being from the transient to the intransient, from the visible to the invisible, from hatred to love. When you experience His love, your earthly life will gain meaning. Your mind will become enlightened, you will perceive the light of the new life and you will begin to understand. Only under such circumstances will you come to know the relation that exists between love and life, between wisdom and light and between truth and freedom. As long as human beings do not become one with Christ, that is, as long as they do not become one with Him in thoughts, feelings, and deeds, the world will not come into order.

I am talking to you about the Living Christ, about that Christ Who bears in His Self life, Who bears the living knowledge and light, Who bears truth and freedom. About that Christ, Who brings all the ways to develop mindful life. He is the Great Christ, Who is called the Head of the Great Universal Brotherhood.

This Christ must be known by people today. It is Him Whom they have to see—to see Him and to know Him. Many people want to convince us that without seeing Christ and without knowing Him inwardly we can be true Christians. However, I say that if one cannot see Christ, nothing can come out of such a person. If you harmonize yourselves with Christ, your consciousness will wake up, you will see Him. Christ is coming into the world with His mindfulness and love. Christ is already coming to the earth to bring divine love for all people. He will teach people to sacrifice self and to love. He brings love, wisdom, knowledge, and freedom. The Light of Christ permeates everywhere!

Notes

[1] The word 'I' (in single quotes) is used to denote the innermost spiritual essence of the human being; we shall refer to the general quality of the 'I' as "'I'-hood". Although these terms may feel somewhat cumbersome in English, they correspond exactly to Rudolf Steiner's use of "Ich" and "Ichheit" in the German. Using 'I' also avoids confusion with the words "self" and "ego". "Self" can refer to more than simply the spiritual essence, including all characteristics that belong to any individual human being. While those familiar with Rudolf Steiner's work understand "higher ego" as a synonym for 'I' in contrast to "lower ego", we have sought to avoid altogether any connotation of the lower nature of "ego" as it is understood by contemporary psychology.

[2] It is necessary to explain in the very beginning the spiritual-scientific methods applied to **received** and develop the present ideas: (i) investigation and research of esoteric texts on a large scale; (ii) spiritual-scientific analysis and comparison of the collected information; (iii) formulating summarized theses and theorems; (iv) applying the principle of correspondence and analogy under the conditions of free imaginative reflections; the culmination of this process is the reception of inspirational thoughts and ideas of a new nature in terms of quality (this is not about imaginative and inspirational consciousness of a purest kind but about certain first steps taken in this direction); (v) reflection, discussion and verification of the newly gathered information in a group, as well as delivering of lectures and preparation of seminars and discussions in a wider circle on evolved themes and ideas; (vi) observation of the causes and consequences in the arisen life of the newly established spiritual-scientific environment; (vii) targeted monitoring whether the newly evolved ideas serve the centralizing Christ principle or the polarizing Luciferic, Ahrimanic influences and whether the newly evolved ideas serve the Michael cosmopolitan aims towards the achievement of unified and global common human spirituality, centered in the Esoteric Christianity.

[3] Also called *the spiritual laboratory of humankind* by Rudolf Steiner. See *GA 54*, 16.11.1905. The formulation "Masters of humanity" is intended to denote generally all the elevated Masters leading humankind, including but not limited to the Masters of

Wisdom specifically referred to in the lecture of 16.11.1905.

[4] See *GA 130*, notes from a speech delivered on 28.11.1911, Stuttgart.

[5] See *GA 93a*, 27.10.1905.

[6] See various places in *GA 45* ('Anthroposophy. A fragment from 1910', Dornach, 1970) and particularly p. 45.

[7] Regarding the twelvefoldness of the earthly 'I'-consciousness and about the fact that the 'I' of a human being has a twelvefold structure, see *GA 170*, 12.08.1916.

[8] This process is exceptionally complex and multi-leveled and is mentioned at various places in Rudolf Steiner's lectures. Some of them in a recommended sequence are: (1) *GA 122*, 22.08.1910; (2) *GA 130*, notes from 28.11.1911, Stuttgart; (3) *GA 102*, 29.02.1908.

[9] See *GA 93a*, two lectures delivered on 9. and 10.10.1905.

[10] See the notes to *GA 93* as well as written answers to questions put by Mrs. A. Brandis on 29.05.1915, *GA 264*, p. 191, Anthroposophic Press, 1996, ISBN 0-88010-434-1.

[11] Known also by the rank of *Masters-Mahatmas*. Often Anthroposophic literature uses the specific word *Masters* for them or the Sanskrit term *Mahatma*. See *GA 130*, 17.09.1911.

[12] See *GA 116*, 25.10.1909.

[13] See *GA 116*, 25.10.1909 and *GA 113*, 31.08.1909.

[14] See *GA 118*, 13.04.1910.

[15] See *GA 117*, 19.11.1909.

[16] See *GA 130*, 4.11.1911.

[17] See *GA 113*, 31.08.1909 and *GA 131*, 13.10.1911.

[18] See *GA 116*, 25.10.1909.

[19] Two lectures of Elisabeth Vreede, 9. and 11.07.1930, in T.H. Meyer, *The Bodhisattva Question.*

[20] See note 23 to Chapter *Star alphabet and the constructional concept of the First Goetheanum*, in S. Prokofieff, *The Twelve Holy Nights and the Spiritual Hierarchies*, Noah, Erevan, 1993, translation in Bulgarian, Daskalov Anthroposophic Publishing House, Stara Zagora, 2004, ISBN 954-495-049-4.

[21] See *GA 93a*, 28.10.1905.

[22] See *GA 131*, 12.10.1911.

[23] See *GA 107*, 22.03.1909.

[24] See *GA 114*, 18.09.1909.

[25] See the answer to Mrs. A. Brandis to questions asked on 29.05.1915, GA 264, p.191, Anthroposophic Press, 1996, ISBN 0-88010-434-1; GA 265, pp. 316-317, SteinerBooks, 2007, ISBN 978-0880106122; GA 266/1, p. 483, SteinerBooks, 2006, ISBN 978-0880106108.

[26] See *GA 131*, 13.10.1911, *GA 116*, 25.10.1909 and *GA 130*, 17-21.09.1911.

[27] See *GA 264*, p. 241, Anthroposophic Press, 1996, ISBN 0-88010-434-1.

[28] See *GA 118*, 13.04.1910.

[29] The text in [brackets] is inserted by the authors for the sake of brevity and clarity.

[30] See *GA 93a*, 01.10.1905.

[31] See *GA 130*, 17.09.1911.

[32] See various places in *GA 130*, e.g. the three lectures delivered on 17, 19, 21.09.1911.

[33] Ibid.

[34] Ibid.

[35] See *GA 114*, 16.09.1909.

[36] See *GA 107*, 22.03.1909 and *GA 113*, 31.08.1909.

[37] See *GA 113*, 31.08.1909.

[38] See *GA 114*, 25.09.1909.

[39] See *GA 113*, 31.08.1909.

[40] See GA 123, 10.09.1910 and S. Prokofieff, The East in the Light of the West vol.1-3, Temple Lodge Press, 2010, ISBN 978-1906999063.

[41] See *GA 130*, 19.09.1911 and 5.11.1911.

[42] See *GA 130*, 18.11.1911.

[43] See *GA 130*, 19.09.1911.

[44] See *GA 130*, 21.09.1911.

[45] See *GA 130*, 19.09.1911.

[46] For ease of reference, each hypothesis is designated by number.

[47] See the memoirs of Maria Todorova, a follower of Master Peter Deunov, *The Sunrise of the White Brotherhood*,(in Bulgarian), Zhiten Class Publishing, Sofia, 1993, vol. 1, p. 280, ISBN 954-799-183-3 – vol. I. This text is not yet translated from the Bulgarian.

[48] See Helena Roerich's works published in Russian, vol. 3, 04.07.1936, and published in English as the Letters of Helena

Roerich. The last two titles were taken from the evangelical descriptions of Christ and are referred to Maitreya. This statement was recorded during an important period with particular historic events of the manifestation of the Bodhisattva Maitreya in the name of the Etheric Appearance of Christ. This is available in English cost-free as a Kindle edition on Amazon.

[49] See the works of Helena Roerich, published in Russian, vol.1 and 2, from 12.04.1935 and 4.11.1935. Available in English cost-free as a Kindle edition on Amazon.

[50] See Adolf Anderson's lecture on the Bodhisattva Maitreya: *Rudolf Steiner und der Bodhisattva des 20. Jahrhunderts (Rudolf Steiner and the Bodhisattva of the Twentieth Century)*, Freiburg 1980.

[51] See GA 123, the end of lecture of 10.09.1910.

[52] Elisabeth Vreede, two lectures on 9. and 11.07.1930, in T.H. Meyer, *The Bodhisattva Question*.

[53] In order to understand such a situation, the reader may examine the two lectures entitled *Rosicrucianism and the Maitreya Buddha. The Bodhisattva - the future Maitreya Buddha* at the following web site: www.anthroposophyinsydney.org/articles.htm. Transcript of two lectures given by Adriana Koulias in August 2003 before an anthroposophical audience.

[54] A similar argument has been put forward by Adolf Arenson in his lecture regarding the 20th century Bodhisattva, but unfortunately, through the circumstances of the time, he did not have sufficient and complete information about whether someone other than Rudolf Steiner had spoken about the Second Appearance of Christ; therefore he arrived at an unfortunately ill-founded conclusion, partly addressed by Sergei Prokofieff. This issue is commented on in greater detail further on in the text.

[55] More on this issue can be found in Lazaridès, Prokofieff, *Трагедия Валентина Томберга*, Strasburg – Sanct Peterburg, 1999 (published in English *as The Case of Valentin Tomberg*, London 1997).

[56] See *Оккултьное замещение Бодисаттвы* (p. 84-85) in Lazaridès, Prokofieff, *Трагедия Валентина Томберга*, Strasburg – Sanct Peterburg, 1999.

[57] The very name of the teaching that drives and inspires this esoteric Christian community of thousands of Bulgarians is the *Teaching of the Universal White Brotherhood*. Secular circles

usually refer to the human community of the followers of Master Peter Deunov as the *White Brotherhood*. This is not a secret occult brotherhood but a powerful social movement with esoteric Christian roots that appeared first in Eastern Europe and afterwards worldwide. It should be emphatically mentioned here that this movement first came into existence in Bulgaria at the beginning of 20th century, and later on, in France, the movement established by Mihail Ivanov, a disciple of Master Beinsa Douno. Afterwards these two centers in Bulgaria and France established a number of units of their own worldwide. This spiritual tradition unquestionably has nothing to do (either methodologically, historically, or in terms of traditions or organization) with the Theosophy of Blavatsky, Besant, and Leadbeater; with the writings of Alice Bailey; with the Roerich family and the so-called Tibetan; with any Western racist organizations; or with local religious pseudo-theosophical organizations and sects appearing in the former Soviet Union or in any of its former republics. Similar organizations, having nothing to do with the esoteric Christian teaching originating in Bulgaria, can be researched by readers themselves: a Ukrainian apocalyptic sect of theosophical eclectic roots leading to several instances of suicide at http://www.usmalos.com/; one of the many cases of a self-proclaimed Messiah-Christ descending physically on the Earth at http://visarion.da.ru/; a racist organization proclaiming superiority and that the white race is chosen by God at http://churchoftrueisrael.com/.

The concepts *White Lodge, White Brothers, White Brotherhood, the Brotherhood of Light* should be understood in the purely spiritual-scientific sense used by Rudolf Steiner and Master Peter Deunov. This is an idea originally given by the two contemporary branches of esoteric Christianity, referring solely to all ten ranks of Angelic Hierarchies, a group of highly evolved Masters and their closest disciples and co-workers, who have Christ as their spiritual center, leader and supreme initiator. We mention this in particular because during the second half of 20th century there were a number of cases when clearly ill-minded adepts and messengers of eastern non-Christianized spiritual organizations or schools of the left [evil] initiation, or mediums performing channeling, who, under the same names have been conducting ideas and concepts completely different from those mentioned above– concepts, ideas and beings who are not related to and have nothing to do with the Christ Spirit. This is aimed at an even greater chaos and 'easy catch' of non-oriented people who are not familiar with the Spiritual Science and who would easily be manipulated by such influences. Moreover, the authors of this study consider this to be one of the many attacks against the activity of the Masters of the White Lodge – the Masters of Wisdom and the Harmony of Sensations and Feelings, and more specifically – one of the many attacks against the Bodhisattva Maitreya appearing in the 20th century.

[58] More details about the life of Mihail Ivanov can be obtained at the official French web site www.fbu.org , in the official Bulgarian web site dedicated to the Word of the Master Peter Deunov (BeinsaDouno.org) or in the book by Louise-Marie Frenette, *Omraam Mikhaël Aïvanhov et le chemin de Lumière*, Editions A.L.T.E.S.S., Paris, 1997.

[59] See *GA 130*, 17.09.1911.

[60] See *GA 130*, 21.09.1911.

[61] See *GA 130*, 27.09.1911.

[62] For instance: *Everywhere you are, I can be addressed, But in your temples best, Address me and you address, Lord Buddha, Address Lord Buddha, then you address Maitreya.* (From *Hymn of Asia*, American Graphics Inc., 1974).

[63] What is meant here is the rhythm described by Rudolf Steiner: a sequence of appearance – activity – stillness (in this case beginning at about the turn of the 20th century); new appearance – activity – stillness. This is repeated similarly every 100 years.

[64] See S. Prokofieff, The East in the Light of the West vol.1-3, part III, pp. 450-451. Temple Lodge Press, 2010, ISBN 978-1906999063.

[65] See *GA 130*, 4.11.1911.

[66] Friedrich Rittelmeyer, the founder of the Christian Community, had several deeply esoteric conversations with Rudolf Steiner and made notes of them which later came into circulation.

Referring to Jeshu ben Pandira as an earlier incarnation of the Bodhisattva who will become the Maitreya Buddha, Rudolf Steiner – in response to a question from Friedrich Rittelmeyer – said: "Jeshu ben Pandira [i.e. the reincarnated Jeshu ben Pandira] was born at the beginning of this century, and if we live another fifteen years, we shall notice his activity."

This remark, made in August 1921, points to a birth in the year 1900 or thereabouts and noticeable culmination of activity in 1936.

[67] See *GA 130*, 01.10.1911; this text is repeated also in *GA 118*, 15.03.1910.

[68] See *GA 131*, 14.10.1911.

[69] See *GA 114*, 25.09.1909.

[70] See Adolf Andersen's lecture about the Bodhisattva Maitreya: *Rudolf Steiner und der Bodhisattva des 20. Jahrhunderts* (*Rudolf Steiner and the Bodhisattva of the Twentieth Century*), Freiburg 1980. Not available in English.

[71] Ibid.

[72] See Rudolf Steiner's particular statement in that regard in *GA 131*, 14.10.1911.

[73] "Meta-analysis is the statistical procedure for combining data from multiple studies." For more about meta-analysis, see, for example, https://www.meta-analysis.com/pages/why_do.php.

[74] See Rudolf Steiner's statements on the Black Sea region and the related spiritual mysteries in *GA 130*, 18.12.1912 and *GA 140*, 18.11.1912.

[75] It should also be noted that Heindel's work is an imitative interpretation of Rudolf Steiner's early lectures rather being self-reliant. This contradicts the indication that the Bodhisattva will not have a relationship as a disciple to a master.

[76] See *The Master in Varna*, (in Bulgarian), compiled by Dimiter Kalev, Byalo Bratstvo Publishing House, Sofia, 1999, ISBN 954-8091-91-7. This is not yet translated from the Bulgarian.

[77] "Slavic" is a contemporary historic term coming from 17th century defining the population speaking Slavic languages. For example: Slavic does not exist in any historic document in the Middle Ages or earlier nor a substitute of "Slavic" term.

[78] See F. Niel, *Albigeois et Cathares*, Presses Universitaires de France, 16ᵉ édition, 2000; translated in Bulgarian: *Albigensians and Cathars*, Cama Publishing House, Sofia, 2003, ISBN 954-9890-50-3. Available in French and Bulgarian only.

[79] More about the Bulgarians and their mission can be found in GA 237, 11.07.1924, and in Markus Osterrieder, "Sonnenkreuz und Lebensbaum, Irland, der Schwarzmeer-Raum und die Christianisierung

der europaeischen Mitte," S. 367, Urachhaus, 1995.

[80] Master Peter Deunov says that the foundations of the Teaching of the Universal White Brotherhood are stated in it.

[81] See *GA 130*, 01.10.1911.

[82] See *GA 114*, 25.09.1909.

[83] From *The Master Speaks*, compiled by Georgi Radev (following texts of Master Beinsa Douno), in *The Great Universal Brotherhood* Chapter. ISBN 954-8785-17-X. Available in Bulgarian only.

[84] The conception *Universe* is understood to mean our Galaxy, the Milky Way. Elsewhere the Master Peter Deunov calls this Central Sun by the name of *Alphiola*.

[85] From conversations with the Master Peter Deunov published by Boyan Boev in the book of *The Good Predisposition*, chapter entitled *The Master about Christ.* ISBN 954-744-026-8. Available in Bulgarian only.

[86] From *The Master Speaks*, compiled by Georgi Radev (following texts of Master Beinsa Douno), in the chapter entitled *Christ.* ISBN 954-8785-17-X. Available in Bulgarian only.

[87] From conversations with the Master Peter Deunov published by Boyan Boev in *The Good Predisposition,* chapter entitled *The Master about Christ,* ISBN 954-744-026-8. Available in Bulgarian only.

[88] Protocols from the annual meeting of the White Brotherhood Chain in Veliko Tarnovo, 11.08.1911, ISBN 954-8139-10-3.

[89] Protocols from the annual meeting of the White Brotherhood Chain in Veliko Tarnovo, 15.-18.08.1912, ISBN 954-8139-10-3.

[90] Protocols from the annual meeting of the White Brotherhood Chain in Veliko Tarnovo, 10.08.1914, ISBN 954-8139-10-3.

[91] *The Awakening of the Human Soul,* a talk from the volume *He was Examining Them,* The Sunday talks series 1923.

[92] From the book of *Fine-tuning of the Human soul,* vol. I, *Master's Path* Chapter, ISBN 954-744-001-2.

[93] See *GA 130*, 21.09.1911.

[94] See the memoirs of Boris Nikolov, one of the closest disciples of Master Peter Deunov, in *The Sunrise of the White Brotherhood* (in Bulgarian), Zhiten Class Publishing House, Sofia, 1995, vol. 3, pp. 77-79, ISBN 954-90041-2-0.

[95] Excerpt from a conversation with Master Beinsa Douno at the home

of Lasar Kotev on 08.08.1920, published in the memoirs and shorthand notes of Boris Nikolov, one of the closest disciples of the Master. Available in Bulgarian only.

[96] See the memoirs of Nestor Iliev, a follower of Master Peter Deunov, in *The Sunrise of the White Brotherhood* (in Bulgaria), Zhiten Class Publishing House, Sofia, 1995, vol. 4, p. 250, ISBN 954-90041-4-7.

[97] J.E. Zeylmans van Emmichoven, *Wer war Ita Wegman?* Vol. 2, p. 222. Heidelberg, 1992: Edition Georgenberg.

In addition, there are anecdotal recounting of a group of Bulgarians approaching Rudolf Steiner and asking him to give lectures in Bulgaria and to found a branch of the Anthroposophical Society in Sofia. Rudolf Steiner is reported to have declined to found such a branch with the words, "No, you have Beinsa Douno". Similar later again Bulgarians approached Marie Steiner von Sivers asking to come to Bulgaria with eurythmy performances and set up eurythmy courses there. Again similar answer. The source of this information comes from Jörgen Smit, deceased member of the board of the General Anthroposophical Society. He expressly confirmed in 1989 that he already knew these stories since he first travelled to Dornach from Norway at the end of the thirties.

[98] See *GA 264*, p. 238, personal communication with Friedrich Rittelmeyer, not dated.

[99] Moreover, Rudolf Steiner visited the Carpathian Mountains in Romania end of 1889 for Christmas time (see his autobiography). He has personal experience of this mountain and cannot mistaken it later on. Some other researchers try to link both mountain regions as one but as per any scientific sources these are two very different mountains divided by the large Danubian Plain. Carpathians are the most south-eastern geographical destination he visited. Rila and the Vitosha Mountains are more than 500 km (300 miles) farther south in Bulgaria.

[100] See *GA 116*, 25.10.1909.

[101] See *Encyclopedia Britannica*, entry under "Essene".

[102] See *GA 130* – lectures delivered on 19.09.1911, 5.11.1911 and 3.12.1911, and *GA 118* – 27.02.1910.

[103] "Cross-cultural research is a scientific method of comparative research which focuses on systematic comparisons that compares

culture to culture and explicitly aims to answer questions about the incidence, distributions, and causes of cultural variation and complex problems across a wide domain, usually worldwide." See the International Journal of Psychological Studies, Vol. 1, No. 2 (December 2009), "What is Cross-cultural Research?"

[104] See *Conversations at the Seven Rila Lakes* (in Bulgarian), Queen Mab Publishing House, 1993, ISBN 954-478-11-3, in the chapter entitled *Universal White Brotherhood through the centuries.*

[105] Rudolf Steiner, *The Secret Stream: Christian Rosenkreutz and Rosicrucianism*, Anthroposophic Press, 2000, ISBN 0-88010-475-9.

[106] The volumes of this series in its most complete edition so far was published in 2006 by the Byalo Bratstvo Publishing House and Zahari Stoyanov Publishing House.

[107] See *GA 346*, 20.09.1924.

[108] See two lectures published in the series *GA 123*, 6. and 10.09.1910.

[109] See *GA 130*, 21.09.1911.

[110] See *GA 114*, 25.09.1909.

[111] The text was published in the above-mentioned notes of Boris Nikolov, in *The Sunrise of the White Brotherhood*, Zhiten Class Publishing House, Sofia, 1995, vol. 3, ISBN 954-90041-2-0. Available in Bulgarian only.

[112] See *GA 116*, 25.10.1909.

[113] The Sixth Epoch will run from A.D. 3573 to A.D. 5733; the mission of the Maitreya will end with his becoming Buddha around the year A.D. 4400 or 4900.

[114] Verbatim indication of Peter Deunov in A Call to my People, Publishing Bialo Bratstvo 2014, ISBN: 978-954-744-237-5. Protocols from the annual meeting of the White Brotherhood Chain in Veliko Tarnovo, from 23.08.1911, Publishing House Zahari Stoyanov and Bialo Bratstvo 2007, ISBN: 978-954-739-987-7. Available in Bulgarian only.

[115] See *GA 237*, 11.07.1924.

[116] Rudolf Steiner has more on this 'musical' method in *GA 283*.

[117] See *GA 116*, 25.10.1909.

[118] See *GA 136*, 7.03.1912.

[119] See *GA 136*, 07.04.1912 and *GA 110*, 16.04.1909. In this lecture, Rudolf Steiner uses the term "Dhyana-Buddha" in the sense that he

uses "Buddha" everywhere else, and he uses the term "Buddha" to denote a human being as a lower level of inspiration than the Bodhisattvas.

[120] See *GA 130*, notes from a lecture on 28.11.1911, Stuttgart, and GA 136, the lecture of 07.04.1912.

[121] Regarding the etheric skeleton, see the notes of the Esoteric Lesson of 29.11.1907 in GA 266-1 and GA 264. Regarding the etheric body as the place where Lucifer and Ahriman meet in the human being, see GA 134, 29.12.1911

[122] See *GA 94*, 09. and 10.06.1906

[123] From the words of the Master Peter Deunov published as an appendix to the *Testament of the Color Rays of Light,* ISBN 954-744-042-X. Available in Bulgarian only.

[124] See *GA 123*, 05.09.1910.

[125] More on the Spirits of Fire and Light can be found in the first several lectures published in *GA 110* and particularly in the lecture of 13.04.1909.

[126] See S. Prokofieff, *The East in the Light of the West,* vol.1-3, Temple Lodge Press, 2010, ISBN 978-1906999063.

[127] From the words of the Master Peter Deunov published as an appendix to the *Testament of the Color Rays of Light,* ISBN 954-744-042-X..

[128] See *GA 110* and particularly the lecture of 13.04.1909.

[129] See *GA 130*, 1.10.1911.

[130] Here one can notice an interesting similarity between the notion of the *Vatan language,* introduced by Master Beinsa Douno with respect to the primary language of humankind, and Rudolf Steiner's ideas on the primary common language of the Atlantis and the activity of the Votan Being – see *GA 101*, 21.10.1907.

[131] The present work only outlines certain ideas and conclusions about Paneurhythmy.

[132] The hula of Hawai'i is an example of such a movement of language.

[133] The following excerpts are from *The Master Speaks*, compiled by Georgi Radev, following the texts of Master Beinsa Douno, in the chapter entitled Christ. ISBN 954-8785-17-X. Available in Bulgarian only.

Made in the USA
Middletown, DE
25 September 2019